Women, Children, Love, and Marriage

by

C. Gasquoine Hartley

Double 9 BOOKS

Women, Children, Love, and Marriage

by C. Gasquoine Hartley

ISBN: 978-93-69079-01-8

Published by

DOUBLE 9 BOOKS

2/13-B, Ansari Road
Daryaganj, New Delhi – 110002
info@double9books.com
www.double9books.com
Tel. 011-40042856

ABOUT THE AUTHOR

Catherine Gasquoine Hartley, also known as C. Gasquoine Hartley or Mrs. Walter Gallican, was a writer and art historian renowned for her expertise in Spanish art. Born in 1867 in Antananarivo, Madagascar, she later became a significant figure in the field of art history, contributing to the understanding of Spanish art in particular. Hartley’s intellectual curiosity expanded beyond art, and she wrote on subjects such as polygamy, motherhood, and sex education, reflecting her broad range of interests. Throughout her life, she was an advocate for deeper societal reflections, addressing issues that were often considered taboo at the time. She passed away on June 9, 1928, in Guildford, United Kingdom, leaving behind a legacy of both scholarly work and thought-provoking social commentary. She was the daughter of a notable family, although her parents' names are not widely recorded. Hartley's contributions, especially in the realms of social thought and the history of art, helped broaden perspectives in the early 20th century. Her works continue to be of interest to those exploring the intersections of art history, social science, and progressive movements of the period.

CONTENTS

And we won't, we simply *will not* face the world as we've made it, and our own souls as we find them, and take the responsibility. We'll never get anywhere till we stand up man to man and face *everything* out, and break the old forms, but never let our pride and courage of life be broken.

D. H. LAURENCE in "Aaron's Rod."

FOREWORD

The essays here collected were written on various occasions over a considerable space of time. This will account for the diversity in the subjects and for a certain amount of restatement of my own beliefs and position.

I have not thought it advisable to attempt to alter this, since though some of the things I have said before may be repeated, the point of view and special application are in each case different.

Some of the essays have appeared already in various journals, but all have been very carefully revised and altered and the great majority entirely re-written.

In spite of the diversity of the subjects there is a common idea beneath all the essays—a common back-ground of faith. I do not know whether I am justified in my confidence that this idea—this faith is abundantly manifest. If I should try to formulate it into one short statement, I should say it was the responsibility that the old have to the young—the debt that one generation owes to the next.

In my gospel there is one commandment which may not be broken: *Ye shall not hurt a little child.*

C. GASQUOINE HARTLEY.

Merton Park,
March, 1924.

SECTION I
WOMEN

WOMEN AND CATS

In an admirable speech that I heard a few weeks ago, women were likened to cats. I do not remember exactly in what connection, however this does not matter.

But this remark set me thinking—it was not the first time, by many, that I had heard a man sum up the evil characteristics possessed, or supposed to be possessed, by my sex by likening us to cats. I now asked myself was this true? I want to be frank. Let me confess at once that I have come to the conclusion that the speaker was right. Women and cats have many qualities in common. I have another confession to make. When I first thought of this question of women and cats, I am bound to say that I felt that I did not like either cats or women, in fact I was not sure that I didn't dislike them.

But wait, please, my sisters, before you let your anger fall upon me. This knowledge was so wounding to my self-pride that it forced me into an inquiry. I had made a fatal mistake. I soon found the reason of my dislike. I had been thinking of women and cats as a class and not as individuals. I disliked them just as one dislikes the Chinese, Portuguese, pigs or almost any other class of beings thought of collectively. Of course this is absurd, but then nine times out of every ten we are absurd—or unreasonable, which is the same thing, and only by recognising this can we find the truth. Who is there who has never admired some individual cat? Is there any misogynist who has never loved some individual woman?

Before I come to the real subject of this woman—cat likeness, I would like to say that we women are a little tired of being classed *en masse*. We really are growing wearied of hearing about ourselves. We claim to be appraised as individuals, some good, some bad, most of us a compound of good qualities and bad, but not all alike, not collective. We object to this communion of character. I remember talking to a Frenchman about Englishwomen. He said, "By the ones and the twos you are charmantes, très charmantes, but altogether—no—horrible!" This male logic is ridiculous. Men revile us as a class and sell their bodies and souls to us as individuals.

Now let us look further—What are the class-cat qualities that are also the class-woman qualities?

Few subjects are at once so easy and so difficult to approach as this one of woman and also of cat—our tiny, intimate tiger. We may purr commonplaces, or scratch and spit rage, but the illusive individuality of women and cats escapes description. Yes, the more I consider this subject of women and cats the more convinced I am that this likeness is a compliment to my sex. Like Balaam's ass of old those who set out to curse us are made to bless.

For a moment I want you to think of a beautiful kitten, of her brilliant devilry, her perfect curves, the elusive wonder of her unwinking eyes like orange flowers, the delicate nuances of expression in her tail. Now, I want you to ask yourselves the nature of your regard for this perfect animal. You prize her rather for her beauty, than for her friendship. You call her pet, idiotic names, play with her, then go away and forget her.

The kitten grows up, becomes a cat, and old. She ceases to interest you. Her work is now to catch mice—to serve you. Do you think the cat does not feel this change in her mode of life—this too sudden loss of joy, which is forced upon her as soon as she attains her maturity. If you doubt this, make a real friend—not a plaything—of a kitten. We did this once. The kitten passionately loved my husband; when he went walking she went part of the distance with him; often she waited for him, or watched for his return loudly purring a welcome. Then my husband proved faithless; the kitten grew old and less beautiful, and we got a dog; he ceased to notice her. That cat died; yes, slowly pined away from grief. I acknowledge all cats are not so sensitive; they have not been made friends. The common cat develops an immense power of ignoring your past passionate and playful petting. She becomes distantly indifferent, or coquettishly variable—purring at one hour, scratching at another. She remembers her past; she understands what you valued in her. All that is herself she keeps for herself.

Contrast the cat with the dog. The blind worship of the one, the exquisitely calm indifference of the other. The dog accepts you, whatever treatment you give him, because you have loved him for himself—made him your companion, your friend. But can you expect this from the cat? You have never made her your friend; you have not found it worth while to understand her. She deceives you. She scratches you with those exquisite velvet paws do you annoy her. You cannot teach her not to thieve. But why? She has no other weapon, and the great life force urges her to self-protection.

And how splendidly she defends herself; how persistent and how successful she is in gaining her desires. And how well she understands the advantages that beauty gives to her; advantages she can gain from nothing else. There is something really splendid in the trouble the cat takes over her personal attire; to keep the seductive whiteness of her shirt front's pretty fur, the glossy shine of her splendid tiger skin. The dog would be quite happy and proud when dirty—ugliness is allowed to him. But the cat!—only when her self-respect is dead can she neglect to be beautiful.

Yes, now I have come to think about cats, I am filled with adoration. With every force against her the cat has kept her power! Her rudeness is sublime! Her aloofness is adorable! You may scratch her chin, she will permit this if she feels inclined, but the allowing of this familiarity does not forward your intimacy with her in the least—she knows what your advances mean. Sometimes she will not respond to your supplications—you cannot compel her. She wishes to sit upon your lap, a dozen times you send her down and each time she returns; you want her to sit upon your lap, and a dozen times she refuses and jumps down. She imposes her will upon you with a lordship that admits of no dispute. The personality of the cat is persistent and overwhelming, she is inconceivably herself. Nothing living—no, not even woman—is so self-supporting—I do not mean this economically, but artistically,—and self-centred as the cat. She is the great ego—the supreme type of the Super-Me.

I have said almost nothing at all about the character of woman. Is it necessary? I think not.

THE WOMEN OF SPAIN

Wherever I go in Spain, in the streets of the towns, in the churches, in the work-rooms, I am impressed with the fine types of the women; their strength and quietness—the same quality which Valeria, the Spanish novelist, speaks of as "a notable robustness."

There is a fascination about Spanish women not easy to define. Not all of them are beautiful, and it is, of course, easy to find women of all degrees of ugliness, but the proportion of those who are strong and beautiful seems to me to be very large. There is greater variety of types in northern than in southern Spain. While there are many women who are dark, with golden complexions, and quite Arabian eyes, a proportion of fair women will be found with bright brown, auburn, and some, even golden hair. One sees rosy complexions and blue eyes that remind one of England; though mixed grey eyes are more frequent. Many of the faces have finely modelled features, quite classic in outline. Certainly the most beautiful and distinguished faces are not found among the women of the so-called upper classes, but belong to the fish-girls and market-women of the towns and the peasants of the rural districts. And this presence of a really fine type among the workers of a race is a certain indication of an old civilisation.

Many of the women workers in northern Spain are singularly individual. They are usually tall, and have very distinct features, especially the nose. It is a face in which every line has character, much strength, and also humour, rising quickly to the beautiful eyes, but slowly to the mouth, lengthening it into a smile. They all look like women whom no man could venture to insult. I do not know whether one must attribute it to their dress—the vivid coloured handkerchiefs which set their faces, as it were, in an Oriental frame—but these women have a serious, passionate look, which is completely fascinating. They are different from the women of southern Spain, who are smaller, more graceful, perhaps more piquant, but certainly less beautiful.

Living in Spain, you come to understand that this land is really the connecting link between Europe and Africa. Both in their physical traits and in their character, the Spaniards show their relation to the North African type; seldom, indeed, is a Spaniard entirely a European. And it is amongst the women that the resemblance stands out most clearly. There are women with dark long African faces. You will see them among the *flamencos* of Seville or in the gipsy quarter of the Camino del Sacre-Monte at Granada,—women with slow sinuous movements, which you notice best when you see them dance, and wonderful eyes that flash a slow fire, quite unforgettable in their strange beauty. In dress you still find the Oriental love of bright and violent colours. The elegant Manilla shawls and the mantillas which give such special distinction to the women of southern Spain, are modifications of the Eastern veil. The elaborately dressed hair, built up with combs, with one rose or carnation giving a note of colour, has also a very ancient origin.

Racial types may nearly always be best studied in the women of a nation, and this is certainly so in a very old civilisation like Spain, where many forces have combined to waste the men of the race. Representing as they do both on the physical and psychic side a conservative tendency, and with a lower variational aptitude than men, women preserve more markedly primitive racial elements of character. This may possibly explain why the women of Spain, on the whole, are finer than the men.

How well I recall these women as I have seen them often, gathered for the morning markets in the towns; chaffering, laughing, and carrying on their work in the conversational Spanish manner. Here is commercial activity united with a picturesque beauty, unspoilt by the usual ugliness of business. Ugliness is not a necessary growth of progress. There is terrible poverty in Spain. The peasants in the country and the labourers in the towns suffer much injustice in too heavy rents and an unfair burden of taxation. But as I have come to know them, I have realised that the sum of their poverty is, after all, so much less than the sum of their knowledge of the art of living. Not their poverty, but their splendid capacity for eluding its misery, is what is so remarkable. These workers have colour not only in their dresses, but in their souls.

I see again a charming scene that I chanced upon one day in the beautiful town of Vigo, which is situated in Galicia, in the extreme north-west, and is one of the seaports by which the stranger enters Spain. The day was saddened with heavy rain; a company of girls, who had just finished their work of packing the fish for market, had gathered in two empty railway vans, and were dancing together, in the most delightful way, watched and applauded by a group of youths.

It was a dance of quick movement and of great variety. It was not a dance of the feet only, every part of the girls' bodies played its part in the performance, the swaying figures, the beckoning hands, the glittering smiles, that came and went in their dark eyes—all contributed to the dance, which like all Spanish dances was a love drama of intense passion; but always decorous, always beautiful. And the watching youths took their part by a rhythmic clapping of hands and stamping of feet. There was something infectious in this spontaneous gaiety. These girls, I felt, understand happiness, and, as I watched them, the world seemed once more a place in which workers could have their share of the joy of living.

Nor does this overflowing and joyous vigour belong to youth alone. I have seen mothers, stout and matronly, at play in the national games, throwing large heavy balls of wood along the grass with a healthy pleasure in muscular movement. Women, no longer young, may as often be seen dancing as the girls. Well, I remember one woman; she was quite old, and her skin was a yellowed mass of wrinkles. But the wrinkles on her face were but the work of time and the hardness of living, and went no deeper than the skin; they had not touched her soul. She was a little bowed, yet she held herself finely, as indeed, do all Spanish women. I shall never forget her perfect absence of self-consciousness; her abandonment as she quivered all over with the excitement of the dance—and she used her castanets with the innocent coquetry of a young girl. There is something that may well give thought in this wholesome energy, which is so abundant as to find its expression in play.

If I have emphasised the physical qualities of the women workers of Spain, it is because I regard these qualities as being the outward expression of intelligence and will. It is true that Spanish women are not educated as we count education; many of them cannot read or write. But in no other land can women be found with a finer understanding of all that is essential in womanhood.

From the earliest notices we have of Spanish women we find them possessed of a definite character of remarkable strength. Courage and strength have throughout the centuries been common qualities among Spanish women. The history of the *mujeres varoniles* of this land would fill a volume: women who would take the field and fight with a sagacity and ferocity equal to, and often surpassing, that of men.

We may still associate the position of women with some of the old traditions. Women are held in honour. Many primitive customs survive, in particular among the Basques; and one of the most interesting is that by which in some districts a daughter takes precedence over the sons in inheritance of land and family property. As far back as the fourth century, Spanish women insisted on retaining their own names after marriage, for we find the Synod of Elvira trying to limit this freedom. The practice is still common for sons to use the name of the mother coupled with that of the father, and even in some cases alone, showing the absence of preference for paternal descent. Velazquez, for instance, is known to the world only by the name of his mother: his father's name was de Silva. It is significant that in no country does less stigma fall on a child born out of wedlock; and the unmarried mother meets a recognition that is rarely accorded to her elsewhere. I questioned a cultured Spaniard on the position of the prostitute; his answer is worth recording, "Our women give themselves for love much more often than for money." This statement may have some extravagance, but I believe it corresponds to a real fact in the position of women, which persists from a time when their liberty was greater than it is to-day. The introduction of modern institutions, and especially the empty form of chivalry, has lowered the position of women. Emilia Pardo Bazan, the great woman novelist of Spain, has said, "All the rights belong to men, and the women have nothing but duties." Yet there can be no question that some features of mother-right have left their imprint on the domestic life of Spain, and that women have in certain directions preserved a freedom and privilege which in England have never been established, and only of late claimed.

The industrial side of primitive culture has always belonged to women, and in many provinces in Spain the old custom is in active practice, owing to a shortage of men through military service and widespread emigration.

The farms are worked by women, the ox carts driven by women, the seed is sown and reaped by women,—indeed, all the work is done by women. And the point to notice here is that the women have benefited by this enforced engaging in activities, which in most countries have been absorbed by men. The fine physical qualities of these workers is evident. I have taken pains to gain all possible information on this question. Statistics are not available because in Spain they have not been kept from this point of view. It is, however, the opinion of many eminent doctors, who were questioned by a Spanish friend for me on this subject, that this labour does not damage the health or beauty of the women, but the contrary, nor does it prejudice the life and health of their children.

I have seen many charming scenes of labour; and among my memories a visit I paid to a sardine factory in the town of Vigo stands out clearly. The work-rooms open directly on to the bay; here the boats come, the fish are landed and the silver heaps are washed. The airy rooms were scarcely redolent even of fish; and the most scrupulous cleanliness was evident. They were filled with girls, women, men, and boys. I learnt that both the women and men are well paid, and that there is no separation between the tasks allotted to the two sexes. Women and men labour together side by side, capacity alone deciding the kind of work done. The day's work is the eight hours, established in Vigo by arrangement between the masters and the workers; but when a large catch of sardines comes in it must be dealt with at once, and the workers are then paid overtime on a higher scale than their weekly wages. I saw many ingenious and labour-saving machines, one, which was worked by a boy, made the keys for opening the tins at the rate of 140 a minute. I learnt that most of the machinery is supplied by Germany. I was interested to hear that the waste pieces of tin, left from cutting the boxes, were shipped to that country, to be used for making toys. It was not, however, in these things that I found my chief interest. What I chiefly remember was the fine appearance of the women. I was impressed with their smiling and contented faces. Many of them are mothers, and there is an admirable créche in connection with the sardine factory, where the children are cared for. A more industrious and charming scene of labour it would be impossible to find. I lost no opportunity of inquiry into local industrial conditions. The workers in this town are in a very favourable position, and in many respects Vigo has attained to a degree of humane development under industrial life, which other countries are toiling to achieve.

As workers the women are most conscientious and intelligent, apt to learn, and ready to adopt improvements. From my personal observations I can bear witness that their cottages, though very poor, are usually clean, and their children are universally well cared for. Nowhere are children happier or more loved than in Spain. The women are full of energy and vigour even to an advanced age. They are certainly healthy. I once witnessed an interesting episode during a motor-ride in the country districts of the north. A robust and comely Spanish woman was riding *a ancas* (pillion fashion) with a young *caballero*, probably her son. The passing of our motor frightened the steed, with the result that both riders were unhorsed. Neither was hurt, but it was the woman who pursued the runaway horse; she caught it without assistance and with surpassing skill. What happened to the man I cannot say. When I saw him he was standing in the road brushing the dust from his clothes. I presume the woman returned with the horse to fetch him.

Women were the world's primitive carriers. In Spain I have seen women bearing immense burdens, unloading boats, acting as porters and as firemen, and removing household furniture. I saw one woman with a chest of drawers easily poised upon her head, another woman bore a coffin, while another, who was old, carried a small bedstead. A beautiful woman porter in one village carried our heavy luggage, running with it on bare feet without sign of effort. She was the mother of four children, and her husband was at the late Cuban war. She was as upright as a young pine, with the shapeliness that comes from perfect bodily equipoise. I do not wish to judge from trivial incidents, but I have found in these Spanish women a strength and beauty that has become rare among women to-day. When a fire breaks out in a small town or village it is the women water-carriers who act as firemen. They fetch the water from fountains and pour it upon the flames. Just recently I have read of three of these women who lost their lives in an attempt to rescue a cripple girl from a burning house.

I was never tired of looking at the Spanish water-carriers; the fountains that are in every town are the most delightful watching-places. The grace with which the women walk on the uneven roads and their perfect skill in balancing their beautiful *jarras* of stone or copper called forth my unceasing admiration. One result of this universal burden-carrying on the head is the perfect and dignified character of the women's manner of walking. These women walk like priestesses who are bearing sacred vessels. They move erectly, but without stiffness, with a secure and even stride, planting the foot and heel together, light and firmly. There is something of the grace of an animal in their movements—the alertness, the perfect balance, the suggestion of hidden strength. I recall a conversation I had once with an Englishman, of the not uncommon strongly patriotic and censorious type. We were walking on the quay at La Coruna; he pointed to a group of women-bearers, who were at work unloading a vessel, and said in his indiscriminate British gallantry, "I can't bear to see women doing work that ought to be done by men." "Look at the women!" was the answer I made him.

It is interesting to contrast the robust heroines of Spanish writers with the feminine feebleness and inanity which so often are the ideal of English novelists. In Spanish literature vigour and virility, are qualities apart from sex and are bestowed on women equally with men.

Again and again the thoughtful reader will be struck with this in the works of the Spanish writers. It is a point of such interest that one would like to linger upon it. I may mention, as one instance, Cervantes' heroines: the "illustre Fregona," "beautiful, with cheeks of rose and jessamine, and as hard as marble," and Sancho's daughter, who was "tall as a lance, as fresh as an April morning, and as strong as a porter." Of Tirso de Molina, the great Spanish dramatist, it has been said that he gives "all vigour to his women and all weakness to his men." Nor has this robust ideal of womanhood changed. We meet the same qualities among the women depicted by the Spanish writers to-day. Blasco Ibanez, in his "Flor de Mayo," describes a young woman who could meet "a stolen embrace with a superb kick, which more than once had felled to the ground a big youth as strong and firm as the mast of his boat." Among the heroines of Juan Valera we find "Juanita" who, "as a girl could throw stones with such precision that she could kill sparrows, and leap on the back of the wildest colt or mule," while Dona Luz "could dance with a sylph, ride like an Amazon, and in her walk resembled the divine huntress of Delos."

It may of course be argued that these are chosen types that cannot fairly be said to represent Spanish women. Yet the Spanish writers are realists in a much truer sense than is understood amongst English novelists, and it must be admitted that the persistence of the same qualities in so many heroines proves a fundamental veracity in the type presented; and from my own experience, I can testify that the women I have known, in their vigour and independence, show the qualities of these portrait women.

The fact can scarcely be passed over that these heroines almost all belong to the country districts, sometimes even to the poorest people, and if, as in the case of "Dona Luz," they spring from a different class, they are, as a rule, illegitimate, combining aristocratic distinction with plebian vigour. This corresponds with my own observations. I have found the women workers more robust and more intelligent than the women of the middle and upper classes.

Nor is the explanation far to seek. The preparation that these women receive for life is far inferior to that of the workers, who co-operate with men, and whose lives are as actively productive, and work as capably performed. The women of the richer classes lead lives of marked inferiority; without opportunity for work, and compelled to an existence of restricted activity, it is impossible to develop their physical and intellectual qualities.

Most of these ladies, except when quite young, are stout, they are less intelligent than the peasants, and few of them have ever appealed to me as being beautiful. I hasten to add, however, that they all have the fascination that belongs to Spanish women; a charm not easy to define. I have spoken of this quality before, let me try to make it clearer now. I believe it is that all these "senoras" and "senoritas" understand that they are women, and instead of this bringing them unhappiness and causing, as it so often does, the indefinite unquietness that characterises so many English and American women, you feel that they are glad that this is so. This is why they are so attractive. Spanish women are in harmony with themselves, which gives them something of that exquisite appeal which belongs to all natural things. This is the reason too, why the older women are so good-humoured, smiling and gay; they have none of them missed their womanhood.

Here is the real reason of the admiration which these women so universally arouse,—as women they are so perfect. This is a question that reaches very deeply; it is a quality so easy to see, so difficult to explain. What I wish to make clear is that the modern English ideal for women leaves a wide margin open to desire; the innermost forces of life too often are left unsatisfied, while the women of Spain, with all their restrictions, know what it is that, after all, really brings happiness for women. Which is the wiser knowledge?

The restrictions for women will pass with the expansion of modern life, and then the strong personality of Spanish women, their energy and good sense, will inevitably find expression when opportunity is given to them. But never can they fall, in pursuit of outside things, into the error of forgetfulness of their womanhood. There does not appear to be any vagueness in the souls of these women: our women have so often too much. In the composed presence of the Spanish ladies I have felt that it is little profit to a woman if, in gaining the world, she should lose herself.

THE DANGEROUS AGE

A TRACT FOR THE TIMES

I

Under this title the Danish writer, known as Karin Michaelis, in the far-back years before the war—a time now marked as the terrible period of the suffrage craze, gave to the world a remarkable and intimate revelation of a woman. It is perhaps the most illuminating work that has been written in recent years about women, from its rare quality of femininity, expressed with an unconscious sincerity and biting truth.

It is very late in the day to describe a book which, though now forgotten, was, at the time of its publication, very widely read and still more widely criticised and discussed in almost all European countries. It appeared at a time of great feminist unrest, which accounts, to some extent, for the reception it gained.

The story matters very little, for it is not as the confession of one woman that "The Dangerous Age" gains its importance, it is because it affords a diagnosis of an old and a very great evil, as well it is an acute observation of a certain type of woman's soul or character.

It is from this aspect that I wish to approach it, and for this reason I have called it "A Tract for the Times."

Thus it is of very little importance to my present purpose that the book is not a new one. It does not matter if the story is remembered, or indeed, if the book itself has, or has not, been read. If the reader will recall to his or her mind any one of the restless, unsatisfied women they must know—women, not young but not old, they will have the history (the variety in the details will not matter at all) of Elsie Lindtner, the heroine of this story.

This admirable piece of observation deals with a section of women who have come into being through our industrial civilisation with its wrong ideals and stupid customs. Marcel Prévost 1 in his preface to the book, speaks of Elsie Lindtner's confession as a revelation of the feminine soul of all time. With the latter part of this opinion I entirely disagree. Rather would I say that it is a revelation of the soul of woman as that soul has been evolved through the repression of natural instincts and the want of satisfying fields for the expression of energy, in an atmosphere which very surely gives birth to the modern demons of confused desires and unconscious unhappiness.

The title of the book is not, I think, well chosen. The Dangerous Age—Elsie Lindtner was forty-two when she wrote her confession—was dangerous because of the life which had preceeded it. There is, without doubt, a cleavage in life, which may be said to be marked by the diminishing of attraction towards the opposite sex. But this is common to men as well as to women. It belongs to no special age, and its proportion of danger to the individual rests, first on the fulness or poverty of experience before this period arrives, and secondly on the power to extract from the past the joyous impulse for continuous living. But to Elsie Lindtner, as to all women of such false and restricted experience, it was far more than a cleavage, and because she had never lived simply and completely, she experienced that emptiness which strikes the soul with death when the consciousness comes that the opportunities of life are passing.

The terror of approaching age robbed her of all her hope of future happiness, just because she had emptiness in her past.

It is easy to condemn her, to speak of her selfishness, her falseness, her colossal egoism—there are few adjectives of condemnation that I have not heard applied to the Elsie

Lindtner's of life. Yet if we look at the matter rightly, rather ought we to admire her for the perfect self-sacrifice with which she pursued the one occupation.

II

The question at its root is one of right functioning. For mark the real point of Elsie Lindtner's history is this: all her actions were based on search for pleasure. To gain the possessions of this world was the fixed aim for which she bartered her soul. What does she tell us in one of her letters? She is writing of her school-days. A class mate had said to her, "Of course, a prince will marry you, for you are the prettiest girl here." She carried the words home to a maid who added to the poison:

"That's true enough," she said, "a pretty face is worth a pocketful of gold."

"Can one sell a pretty face, then?" the child asked.

"Yes, to the highest bidder," was the answer given.

The seed thus sown gave a rich harvest. Sex-trade became the object, which Elsie Lindtner pursued with the same unflinching purpose which directs all those who create for themselves the false gods of possessions. Truly, while we support with our praise the successful financier, we cannot in justice give less esteem to the woman who pursues the same end in the way that is the easiest and surest of success.

It is no part of my purpose to give a resumé of the history of Elsie Lindtner. The details matter little; a structure of life built on a false foundation must of necessity fall to ruin. And there is another point I wish to make clear. The destroying penalty paid by this woman for the gain of wealth and position was a failure of the power to love. The real explanation of her unrest, hysteria, and manifold symptoms of excitement was caused by the unceasing warfare within her of two antagonistic forces—the desire for comfort and ease, partly instinctive, but also fixed by habit, strengthened by a wish to keep the moral dignity imposed upon women by the conditions of the society in which she lived, fighting with the deeply instinctive desire for satisfying sex experience to fulfil the functioning of life.

It is necessary for women to speak plainly. You cannot deny the needs of the body, or prostitute their use, without the soul paying its penalty. That is what women too often forget. A false purity held Elsie Lindtner from giving herself to her lover, Jorgen Mallthe, and kept her faithful in the letter of the law to the husband she had married for his wealth. She had no children. I say without any doubt that she would have been a purer and a better, because a happier and more healthy woman, if she had followed the cry of her heart, at the first, as she was driven in the end to want to do—when it was too late. That she did not do this, but chose to sacrifice her lover in the same way that she had sacrificed her husband must, in my opinion, be counted as sin against her. Only the falseness which had wrapped her own life in a net of pretence could have made her fail to see the truth for herself.

It is a fact of very special importance that Elsie Lindtner and all the women who enter into this book belong to the Scandinavian race, among whom chastity was extolled as the chief virtue of a woman, while any lapse was punished with terrible severity. If the husband of an ancient Dane discovered his wife in adultery he was allowed to kill and castrate her lover. "There is a city," says the Scandinavian Edda, "remote from the sun, the gates of which face the north, poison rains there through a thousand openings, the place is all composed of the carcasses of serpents. There run certain torrents, in which are plunged the bodies of the perjurers, assassins, and those who seduce married women. A black-winged dragon flies incessantly round and devours the bodies of the wretched who are there imprisoned." Again, the Icelandic Hava Maél contains this caustic apophthegm "Trust not the words of a girl, neither to those which a woman utters, for their hearts have been made like the wheel that turns round; levity was put into their bosoms. Trust not to the ice on one day's freezing, neither to the serpent which lies asleep, nor to the caresses of her you are going to marry."

III

Now, it may be asked: What has all this to do with Elsie Lindtner? My answer is: "Everything!" The customs of a past social life do subsist beneath the surface of modern society; we cannot without strong effort escape from the chains of our inheritance. In the sad nations of the cold north, where the natural joy of the body has been regarded as something to be fought with and denied, a perpetual confusion has arisen at the very source of life. For the sex-passion is a force, huge and fateful, which has to be reckoned with. Woman is more primitive, more intuitive, more emotional than man. And the outlets allowed to her in the past have been more restricted; thus the price she pays for any repression of the natural rights of love is heavier. Elsie Lindtner's history is a sermon to all those who set up the false god of chastity for women.

I am aware that this statement will arouse opposition—especially in women. To-day we hear much talk, and often among women who are working nobly for the better life for women, of control of sex and the need of imposing on men the same code of repression which for so long has been imposed upon them. This is, of course, very natural, but that does not make it wise. It is a truth realised by few women that repression is not, and never can be, control. There seems to be a very widespread opinion that to use the divine gift of sex even in marriage, for joy, is wrong. One would be inclined to laugh, if the sadness of this falsehood did not make one want to weep.

The whole subject, wide as life itself, escapes anything like adequate treatment. The lady—the Elsie Lindtners of society—the household drudge and the prostitute, are the three main types of women resulting in our so-called civilisation of to-day, from the process of the past, and it is hard to know which is the most wretched, which is the most wronged, the most destructive, and the furthest removed from that ideal woman which a happier future may evolve.

What, then, in conclusion, is the lesson to be learnt from this "Tract for the Times?" Women must be free—free to work and free to love. Then, and then only, can they claim to be the fitting mates of men, then and then only, will they be able to fulfil aright their supreme work as the mothers of the sons and daughters of the race. This is the path along which freedom is to be found. What, then, is the individual woman to do? This question is one which women at the present have to answer for themselves. But one thing is certain—they must have the courage to tear from their eyes the old and the new bandages that have kept them, and still keep them, in the darkness of ignorance; better even to sin and know the truth than to live in falsehood and in a child's world of pretence.

THE LEGAL POSITION OF THE MOTHER

In spite of the rapid advance that has been made, the legal disabilities of women are still great. Especially is this so in their relationship to their children.

Here where they should be supreme women have really no rights at all under our laws.

They are not the legal parents of their own children. Only if their child is illegitimately born, have they any rights of guardianship. The law recognises the father as the one parent. He is entitled to the custody of the children. He alone can say where they shall live or how they shall be brought up: he alone has the legal right to decide how they shall be educated or what religion they shall follow. No promise that he makes, either before or after marriage is binding. The man may change his mind at any time. The woman has no remedy. It is evident how terrible a force for evil these rights may easily become in the hands of an unscrupulous or vindictive man. If, for instance, the woman does not choose to live where the husband directs, he may take her children from her. Again, if there is any difference of opinion between the two parents the opinion of the one parent—the father, must prevail. And this is so even when the mother, and not he, is the supporter of the family.

And the injustice continues even after death. The father has the right to appoint a guardian to act with the mother, but a guardian appointed by the mother can act only after both parents are dead. The children have to be brought up according to any wishes expressed by the father or even which it is inferred he has intended to express. This is especially apt to cause trouble with regard to religion. Any relation of the father (even when he himself has been either indifferent or irreligious) may claim to have a woman's children trained, *against her wishes,* in the religion professed by the father's family on the ground that the father was nominally a member of that church.

Of course, when there is agreement between the parents, as happily is the case in the great majority of marriages, the law does not matter. Indeed very few mothers have any conception of their position under the law. That is the only reason why these horrible and out-of-date laws have not been repealed.

Fortunately they are unlikely to remain a dark blot upon our statute book. An admirable Bill has been formulated under the direction of the National Union of Societies for Equal Citizenship, which will remedy this long-standing injustice. It has the long title of the Guardianship, Maintenance, Custody and Marriage of Infants Bill. Its two great objects are:—

(1) To make the mother as well as the father the legal parent of her children.

(2) To impose upon both fathers and mothers the liability to maintain their children according to their means.

There are many further admirable provisions, as for instance, the one which gives both parents equal rights in appointing guardians. Where the child is under 16 and has no property, present or expectant, the case may be dealt with in Courts of Summary Jurisdiction (or Police Courts). This is most important, as it makes the benefits of the equal guardianship possible to the working classes, which would not be so, if cases, as at present, had to be heard in High Courts or County Courts.

I shall not trouble to answer the few determined obstructionists who have opposed this Bill. They say that it will cause difficulty in the home, and provide a reason for quarrel between husband and wife. I have too high an opinion of men and women and of their love of their children to believe this. The cases of dispute, sufficiently serious to be brought into the courts, will always be comparatively few. And a decision of justice will be much easier when the partners have an equal status. Then the welfare of the children will be the decisive factor and not as now, the desires of the parents.

Equal guardianship laws are in operation already in many countries: and wherever they have been established they have worked excellently and must be regarded as a complete success.

PROBLEMS OF BIRTH CONTROL

It is generally admitted that there is much to be gloomy about in these days of bad trade and post-war morals. And yet, perhaps, the poor old world does improve in some respects.

One of the most hopeful signs of this improvement to me is the very widespread interest that has been taken of late in birth control. Conferences are held, law-suits are fought and won; pamphlets are written and in almost every town lectures are given, and everywhere groups of earnest-minded people come together to discuss and to learn. Our sense of responsibility has been quickened in connection with birth and the bringing a new life into the world. In a deeper and more practical way we have come to know that no child should be born *unwanted*.

Now, possibly all this suggests no very great moral advance to you. It may be that you regard it as wrong to regulate births in any way. Yet surely it is well for this difficult problem to be carefully considered in open discussion. To avoid error we must have knowledge. For myself, as I have listened to speakers or read of what is being done, though possibly I am in sharp opposition to much that is believed and advised, yet always I am glad when I reflect that only a little while ago the very mention of birth control would have been impossible at any public meeting, nor would any paper have noticed it.

Everywhere since the war the increased interest in the question has been astonishing. Is it, I have asked myself, that the terrible loss of life has forced us at last to have a deeper understanding of the value of life? Certainly all over the world women and men are beginning to understand the right of every child to be well-born.

The relations between the poverty of the family and its size must be considered in connection with this question. Much stress is also rightly laid on the injurious effect on the mother of continuous and unwilling child-bearing, and on the resulting terrible wastage of life in mis-carriages and still-births. Personally, I should always like to hear more of the effect on the children unfortunate enough to live. *For the child is unfortunate who is born into a home unwanted by its mother.*

To give life well it must be given gladly. There can be no deeper tragedy than an unwilling motherhood.

The moral and religious aspects of family limitation have to be considered. It needs to be emphasised how more and more religion to-day refuses to divorce the spiritual from the material necessities of man, and how it begins to appreciate that the bread-and-butter difficulties of life have the greatest effect on the moral character of the people.

If a criticism on the work of those who advocate birth control may be offered, it is that too much time is spent in saying what everyone agrees with. Propositions, which all who think at all practically accept, are gravely supported with elaborate arguments. More might be accomplished if these elementary questions were left and freer discussions given to the many grave problems which still await investigation. There are so many questions on which far more knowledge needs collecting before any definite conclusions of permanent value can be accepted.

Roughly classified, birth control needs to be studied from three different aspects:—

First, there is the effect upon the married couple.

Second, there is the effect upon the child.

And lastly, there is the effect of voluntary limitation of the birth-rate upon society.

In estimating the consequences to the man and the woman, it is impossible to neglect the psychological results.

The effect upon the mind is far stronger and more lasting than any more direct result. I mean, it is what the individual woman or man *feels* about limitation that is important for them. It is their own attitude to what they do that will mainly decide the results it will have. This is a question of the deepest complication. And much more knowledge is needed, and the greatest care is called for not to form hasty and unproved opinions. It is, I must insist, an individual question that can never be arbitrarilly decided, even by those competent to form a decision. That is why so much that is said, even by doctors who ought to know better, is so absurd.

Much easier to estimate is the effect upon the child. Here we seem to be on firmer ground. To save the unwanted child from being born or conceived by drunken or syphilitic parents is a work of such plain morality that there would appear to be no room for difference of opinion.

Yet the question is deeper and far more difficult than this; there are, indeed, a whole group of problems connected with it. There is, for instance, the case of the only child, who always suffers grave disadvantages, brought up in a home with adults.

Again the childless or one-child marriage is often not happy for those who love children. This is felt, in particular, when one partner desires children and the other refuses to have them born. And it must not be forgotten that all that affects the parents, must also have its results on any child that is born. Apart from economic necessities, the small, limited family is, in many ways, harder to bring up than the large family.

With regard to the effect of birth control on society, it is now becoming a familiar reflection that often those least fitted to carry out parental duties, because of faults of character or misfortune of circumstances, have the largest families.

Here the main problem is not so much to teach the mere knowledge of how families are to be limited as to induce that control and to stir up such desire as will lead to limitation being practised.

But of course, the alteration of the characters of men and women is a task of too great difficulty to be treated as a side issue.

Yet I would not end with any word of discouragement. As I started by saying, the mere consideration of these difficult questions in the broad light of day must be felt, by all of us who are old enough to remember the attitude in the past, as a wholesome sign of the times.

We care more, and very slowly we are growing more honest.

SECTION II
CHILDREN

A BOY'S MISERY

Quite the saddest thing I have come across for some time is the account of the suicide from remorse of a widow, who drowned herself in utter misery; her body being found near the spot where a fortnight before that of her son, aged eleven, had been discovered. The boy, it seems had committed suicide after being accused of stealing money belonging to his mother.

Even from the bare outline of what happened there stands out stark, like some haunting fiend of pain, the agony suffered by this boy and mother before each sought the merciful quietness of death.

I find myself conscious of emotion stronger and more vexing than the strangling sense of pity. I am angry at the waste of two lives, and especially of the fine young life so grievously destroyed. Why, I ask myself, do we torture children by forcing on their sensitive natures punishment for failure in right conduct, while we make no attempt to understand the hidden struggles and unexplained emotions that almost always are the cause? How is it we fail to remember so completely our own growth, the mistakes we made, the undiscovered sins that now we have forgotten?

This boy stole from his mother. A thief you call him—a bad and ungrateful son.

But wait—think! Why did he steal?

An easy question, perhaps, you will say to answer. He desired to buy sweets, wished to visit the cinema; he had been betting with his marbles and getting into bad habits; or he wanted to swagger as a capitalist among his friends. Yes, that sounds probable enough; some such were, I expect, the reasons given by the mother, probably believed in by the boy himself. For so often we force the acceptance of our adult stupidities upon our children. The poor boy counted himself a thief, believed that he had sinned; he felt that he had wronged the mother whom he loved so much. He did not know, for there was no one to tell him, that he did not care at all for the money he stole for these trivial reasons. No, he did not know. But underneath, hidden in the darkness of his young soul, there was a stronger driving imperative, unknown and unsuspected by any one, most of all by the boy himself, which was the irresistible force that caused him to steal.

The reason of his action is really simple and would be recognised at once by any psychologist. It must be sought in the relation of the boy to his mother. He was not loved enough. At least, in some way, he was unhappy in his home relationship—at conflict in his innermost nature. He stole money, though, he did not know it, because he wanted love.

Of his life, through his eleven years, I lack the information that would provide us with the necessary details of proof. It is exceedingly improbable that the details will be forthcoming, for this boy was unknown and his death even at the time, caused no stir. But it is a very certain inference from the evidence of the excessive remorse that drove him to take his own life that, sometime in his earlier years, he had suffered some shock of jealousy or stress of misery in relation to his mother, that initiated the trouble, which later had to force an expression by means of his thefts.

I hope that I make my meaning clear. The idea of "transferring" a feeling into a quite different action may be a little strange to you. Yet everyone knows that, if you are angry with someone and dare not show it, you may gain relief from some kind of violent action entirely unconnected with the cause of the angry feelings. The boy who is afraid of his father, or is otherwise unhappy in his home, is very likely to be a "bully," he takes what he has suffered out of someone weaker than himself. And it is the same process when the suppressed painful feelings of jealousy or other unhappiness take the form of spending money. The impulse is so powerful that if the money cannot be got in any other way, it will be stolen.

In many children there arises jealousy in connection with their home relationships, often without reason, but none the less real to the childish imagination, and this causes them to doubt the parental love that is as necessary to them as the sun to the flower. In its mild and practically harmless form this feeling of being neglected, which few children quite escape, is only occasionally active and remains unrecognised, though it is the frequent cause of irritability, of minor sicknesses and faults in behaviour. The results in aggravated cases are far more important, and cause, not infrequently, such a desperate consciousness of inferiority, with an always pressing sense of wanting something, that there arises an overpowering physical and spiritual necessity for the liberation of the hidden trouble. This relief is found usually in acts of violence, frequently in stealing.

In the case we are considering we see the boy, beyond all shadow of doubt, over-sensitive, the symptoms of the unconscious trouble expressing themselves, on the one side, in an exaggerated feeling of inferiority, and, on the other, in a compelling need to find opportunity for the assertion of power. I do not know just how it happened. Maybe, his mother, who has paid with her life in passionate remorse, was too hindered with the troublesome details of life to be able to cultivate and pick the flowers of love. I cannot know, but *I do know* that in the tender psyche or soul of that poor boy was some terrible need for his mother's love—a want which he did not understand, indeed, of which he was probably wholly unaware. He may even have been in outward rebellion, have thought he was indifferent to his mother, but such a state would but furnish further witness to the trouble within. Had he known what it was he wanted, he would not have done what he did. But the ever-disturbing need, causing confusion in his soul, drove him to steal the most obvious thing that he was without and his mother possessed—that was money.

I do not hesitate to state that in the great majority of cases of boyish thieving the reasons for the act must be sought in some deeply hidden cause, marking some inner disturbance, with a feeling of wanting something which the boy does not understand. The taking of small sums of money or other pilfering acts is a covering-mask, and has no connection with crime. There is one thing further that it is necessary to remember. Though the fault of boyish thieving is not in itself a sign of any moral failure in the character, our treatment of such small thefts—our adult stupidity in understanding the difficulties and seeking out the concealed unhappiness of the young soul, often hounds on the stealing boy into the thief.

We make criminals of the young because we are blind and hardened with our own failures and minor struggles. We also cause, as in the case of this boy who killed himself, the most heart-breaking tragedies. It is appalling even to contemplate the suffering brought quite uselessly upon boys and girls by grown-up foolish ignorance.

We show too little imagination in our treatment of the child who does wrong. We rarely remember his almost terrible sensitiveness, nor do we consider the unusual advantage (from the point of view of the child) that we possess just in being grown-up. And nothing, as I have said before, is to the boy plainer as a sign of this grown-up freedom than the power we have (or rather that they think we have) to spend money how we like and when we like. That is why the taking of money is one of the most common symbolic acts for a boy's wish for love or power.

That boyish theft is often pathological is proved by the fact that the objects stolen are often useless to the boy, that they are hidden away, and, as a rule, forgotten, and further that the boy forgets, or almost forgets, what he has stolen or how he took them. Some boys have a passion for stealing certain objects which they will take over and over again. Those who have had anything to do with delinquent children well know these symptoms.

In nearly all cases the thieving is repeated over long periods; although each act may be followed by violent remorse. Parents and all those who have to deal with these childish wrong doers, should know that this sorrow, especially if it is emotionally excessive, serves only to increase the tendency to a fresh repetition of the theft. For remorse fixes the boy's attention on his stealing, and, still more, on the pleasurable feelings that unconsciously to himself are connected with the act. He remembers these, though he does not know it, whenever he thinks of his wickedness in stealing. And this fixity of attention in itself is a kind of rehearsal of the act, that is very likely to lead to an actual performance of it. Boyish remorse is, no doubt, gratifying to parents, but, almost invariably, it is harmful to the boy.

Whenever the boy thinks how bad he is, how wrong and disastrous an act would be, he is in danger of being compelled to perform that act. Most of us have experienced this, but we forget its application to the moral conduct of the young. Once think how terrible it would be to fall down the precipice, and the idea of jumping down approaches.

Remorse is a form of temptation. And all forms of temptation should, if possible, be avoided in dealing with the misconduct of children. If your boy steals money do not leave money lying about. Also, even if he has stolen money several times, express no faintest suspicion as to his not using honourably any money entrusted to him, for some necessary purpose, such as paying railway fares or buying a school book. Never be suspicious over the change such a child brings you. As he steals from a feeling of inferiority, and, in particular, because through jealousy, whether imagined or real, he feels himself less blessed with the love of those about him than other more confident children, any sign of your not being able to trust him, must render him more liable to err.

If the thieving boy were treated with sympathy and understanding, and loved and helped, instead of being blamed and often cruelly punished, there would be fewer grown-up thieves.

CRIMINALS MADE IN OUR NURSERIES

Every child suffers sometimes from a feeling of inferiority. He is so much smaller and weaker than the grown-ups who control his play and his work that he feels uncomfortably helpless against their authority, which to him seems often to be exercised in an arbitrary and unkind way.

There are times when this consciousness of being little and weak is so overwhelming that the child is bound to do something to convince himself of his own powerfulness.

It is then that he becomes naughty. For the very easiest way to command the attention of his mother, and the other adults who are with him, is by being naughty. Good, he is left alone. The grown-ups go on with their own occupations. He feels neglected. At most he is mildly praised. "Johnnie is a nice quiet boy to-day." But this is very different from the attention he commands when he is naughty. He defies authority. For a short time he becomes a despot, ruling the grown-ups who usually rule him. His sensation of power is intensely enjoyable. And the more disturbance he makes in the nursery life the deeper is his satisfaction. Of course, he is sorry afterwards. But his sorrow is not really for the first period of successful rebellion, but for the following time after his power fails.

Now, it is very important for the mother to understand this. The real problem is to minimise as much as can be of the child's enjoyment of naughtiness.

Any unwisdom on the mother's part such as her being too emotionally concerned, indulging in nagging or violent anger, may have very serious results. Inevitably the child feels as he sees his mother's tears and want of control, "I have caused this." Instead of being weak he is master of his mother. That is why usually he is good after he has been naughty.

But this kind of nursery behaviour is disastrous to the child's character.

Let me tell you a rather striking story to illustrate this. A young boy, very naughty, was sent to bed. His mother, greatly troubled, went some hours later to his room. He was kneeling, praying. She thought he was asking God to forgive him. But this was what she heard: "Please, dear God, forgive my bad mummy for being so unkind to poor little Freddy." The boy grew up in the most unfortunate way. I cannot give the details and there were, of course, several causes. Yet certainly his character suffered the first wrong in the nursery from an unwise emphasising by his mother of his own importance.

The naughty child is always the child over-occupied with thoughts of himself. And his feelings are unhealthily important to him just because he finds himself for some cause at a disadvantage. Parents, unconsciously, but very foolishly, emphasise their children's inferiority; they speak of their weakness, tell them they are too little to do this or that, never realising the danger of what they are doing.

Children must not be subjected to conditions of emotional stress, which increase unnecessarily their inevitable consciousness of inferiority in an adult world. If the parents do not find out and remedy the cause of these feelings (which they ought to know are invariably present whenever a child is naughty) and provide an expression by which the desired power is gained in a right way, let me warn them that they are dangerously limiting their children's chance of a successful and happy life. By connecting pleasure with bad conduct, they are certainly, though they do not know it, making the way easy for every kind of future bad conduct.

The fate of all children is decided in the nursery; criminals are made there as well as saints and heroes.

THE TYRANNY OF PARENTS

In the life of every girl and every boy there come times when they must, and should, free themselves from the thraldom of the home.

This may sound hard to parents, who desire almost always to keep their children in tutelage, and cannot often even think of them except as belonging to the home and to themselves.

Yet the young must rebel, must escape from this too-closely-binding yoke of love. They have to break away from the moorings of safety; to adventure; to find a place for themselves; to get into the world and to establish their own lives as women and men.

We should hear much less of trouble between parents and children if fathers, and especially mothers, could be made to understand that the conflict with their growing boys and girls is not a personal conflict; that it has nothing, or at least very little, to do with the actual situation, and is not directly dependent on anything that either the parents or the children may do or may not do. And this is comforting to parents—it does not mean that their children love them less.

No, the conflict is based on an inescapable psychological opposition. It is the necessity of the young to escape from the tyranny of the old.

The parent's hand is needed to steady the child, while it is unable to stand firmly on its own feet or to guide its own steps; but as the child grows older, it must learn to walk alone. If the mother persists in holding out a hand, never lets the child fall down, she destroys a proper independence and the hand held-out-too-long is used to satisfy the mother's selfish desire; to give her the pleasure she gains from the child's dependence on herself, and not because of any need of the child for help.

You will see the application of this illustration.

emotional solicitude, blocks the narrow passes that lead on to open and independent life.

THE SUPERFLUOUS FATHER

In many homes, where there are children, the father seems a stranger—almost an intruder.

The central figure in the family is the mother. All the details of her life are familiar to the children; she is seen shopping, cooking, looking after the home. The father is a little mysterious; he goes adventuring in the unknown world. He is picturesque and wonderful; an exciting figure that arouses nursery admiration—but he is unnecessary.

At first the mother occupies all the child's attention. She supplies food, comfort, shelter, teaching and brings happiness to the nursery. She is the first love-object and of supreme importance; the starting point of all those interests of the children which lie outside of themselves.

But the other parent—the superfluous father, comes both as interrupter and friend into this mother-child circle. He plays with the children, opens up new delightful ways of interest, brings the movement that children love. But also he is a disturber. He absorbs the mother, draws her attention and care from the children. He upsets the order and balance of the nursery. He almost dethrones the baby.

Thus at a very early age jealousy of the father begins to stir and unsettle the nursery peace. Usually we either treat this childish jealousy as a joke or refuse to admit its presence, but it is deadly earnest to the child itself. If the mother is capricious, varying in her attentions to her husband and to her children, or if she is over-tender and too demonstratively affectionate, this jealousy may, and indeed, must work great and permanent evil.

You see, it imposes a conflict in the exquisitely responsive child, between the emotions of hate and anger and envy born of jealousy, and the emotions of love and admiration and obedience dependent on a sense of the benefits conferred by the father.

It is the duty of the mother so to balance her favours and her love that the rights of the husband and the children are both maintained, and neither side is tempted to be a monopolist.

For it is not only the children who are jealous of the father. Often the father is jealous of the children. And often he has cause. Some women, when once the child is born, regard their husbands solely as the person for providing money necessary for the maintenance of the home. In any other capacity she has ceased to desire him, frankly he is in the way.

The mother type often ceases, after motherhood, to be the loving mate—the wife. There is so little time for love making in a nursery home. The man becomes a superfluity, his demands tend to be delegated to holidays that are planned, but do not often occur.

Nature herself seems to condemn the man in his capacity as father. So delicate is the bond which attaches him to the child as compared with the unbreakable bindings which hold the child to the mother; so readily can he be pushed outside the circle of the family, where, as a member apart, he will inevitably seek his own interests and pleasures.

Now, whether this complete severance happens or not, some conflict between the father and his children, especially between father and sons is almost bound to occur. This is a war which is normal and, indeed, inevitable—far more so than any class-war, any opposition and struggle between the nations.

Have we not read of the solitary polygamous father of the past, the Old Man of the Tribe, who drove his sons out of the horde as they grew up, because in his greed he wanted all the women to be his wives? Much time has passed since then, but these emotions are very old and very strong. Pity and the gentler feelings of civilisation enable the father to accept the son as a member of the family and as a companion instead of a rival. But echoes remain of the old instincts of jealous rivalry.

No science is so difficult or so important as psychology. It is because parents do not understand their own minds or the minds of their children that they make such mistakes. They do not see that some jealousy and opposition in family relationships are inevitable and, in fact, useful. Else the child would never grow up, would always be overwhelmed by its parents.

So do not let us be too alarmed if sons oppose fathers, or if fathers are wanting in sympathy with their sons.

Yet it must be remembered finally, on the other side, that the authority of the father has to be maintained. Superfluous in the family, from one point of thought, his influence is nevertheless of the most urgent importance. Without it a too great dependence on self is fostered at too early an age, which sets up an intolerant and unreasoning hatred of all authority and an inability to suffer any kind of restraint.

The father thus needs to preserve his rights and duties within the home. If women have had to fight for the Vote and the open door to the profession, the father may have to fight for the love of his children and the key to the nursery.

He must refuse to be regarded as superfluous.

THE PERFECT MOTHER

A few weeks ago a shower of sudden rain brought me for shelter into the house of a kindly stranger, who beckoned me in from the position I had taken under the thickly foliaged trees, bordering her garden. She was a woman who exuded kindness. You know the type—opulent in figure, wholesome and ripe, her face beaming in wide wrinkles of pink flesh.

The sudden generous smile of the big mouth showed her the possessor of a real charm. Her eyes had a blue twinkle that attracted laughter. Quite plainly she would be delightful as a mother. For about her was something that conjured visions of nursery fires, of warm, sweet bread-and-milk, of sugar plums after nasty powders, and of kisses and forgiveness given for childish wrong doing, without any unfair bargaining for repentence.

But this woman had no child. Nature does not always, in this matter, act as intelligently as she might. We all know of many Betsy Trotwoods. On the other hand, we find children lavished wastefully—yes, children, swarming in the cold homes of mothers who do not want them—women without understanding of children or any trace of parental passionateness. Do you not recall many modern prototypes of Mrs. Jellaby?

I felt my bowels ache for this woman with her rich and wasted motherhood. Her opulent affections were lavished not, as they should have been, on the tender warm bodies of little children, but on dogs.

Never have I seen so many dogs: they were placed all over the rather small room. Both easy chairs were occupied by a canine seater. There was a mother with new baby-pups in a lined basket before the great fire. Another dog who was sick was in another basket, wrapped in a shawl, on the other side of the fire. The room was stifling, and had a sick, close, doggy smell. And though I am a lover of dogs, I felt disgusted. I really hated those pampered toys, that snarled and snapped and grumbled at me in the most horrible way. Believe me, I am not exaggerating. You could not speak. The whole room was dogs. Enough! Let us leave them and get on to something of greater value.

It was that thought which caught and gripped my attention. This woman's unfilled life. I could not forget it: it stayed with me long after I had left the house—a memory not to be obliterated.

She was forlorn among her dogs. It was a tragedy of waste. I have had so many dreams of the perfect mother that I was stung to anger and impatience to find her, at last here, squandering her affections on a canine brood.

The situation was so plain. This woman needed children, if not of her flesh, then adopted and made her own by the rich fullness of her motherhood.

NOBODY'S CHILDREN

CHILD ADOPTION: A MUCH NEEDED REFORM

It was a short time after I had found "the perfect mother" thus wasted, that there came into my hands the "White Paper" which gives in full the wise and interesting Report of the Committee on Child Adoption. I knew that here was just the very thing that was wanted. Here was shewn the means by which the motherly childless woman and the motherless child could be brought together.

The desire for child adoption has never been stronger than it is at the present time. But I do not hesitate to say that, in the present absence of any law to regulate and safeguard adoption, the position is so set about with difficulties and so pressed with continuous dangers that the practice ought to be actively discouraged. It is dangerous for the adopter and, what matters even more, it is dangerous for the child.

The emphatic and unanimous decision of the Committee was that there is immediate necessity for a change in the law to make the adoption of children legal in this country. Every one who gave evidence was unanimously in favour of adoption in all cases where, for one reason or another, any child could not have the care of its own parents. It is much better for every child to be brought up in a home than in an institution. Not only is it cheaper, but the child benefits far more. But adoption needs to be regulated and legalised. The child is too precious a possession to leave to anyone to do with as they desire.

The report recommends:—

1. That after obtaining the consent of the real parents and the adopting parents, as well as the consent of the child, if he (or she) is over fourteen, all adoption shall be sanctioned by a judicial authority.

2. That confidential official inquiries shall be made from time to time, as to the child's progress and happiness in the adopted home.

3. That the child shall take the adopter's name, and shall have, as far as is possible, the position of a natural child.

This Report was presented in June, 1921. Yet nothing has been done. And what I wish to emphasize with all the power that I have, is the crime of this delay and the urgent need there is for immediate legislation. Children are waiting to be adopted; childless people are waiting to adopt. Surely it ought not to be difficult to frame a simple law that would safeguard the interests of both.

There is little wonder that hitherto adoption has not been popular in this country. One strong reason that has prevented the far-sighted from attempting it is that in England there is no legal method by which adoption can be carried out. And because of this there is, as I have said, too much danger connected with it, as well as not enough certainty of its continuance. For the law grants the foster-parent no recognised control over the child.

There is the ever present fear, increasing as the years pass and the child grows up, lest the natural parent shall come one day and claim the right to take the child away—an injustice specially likely to happen as the child becomes older and is able to earn money.

Then there is, on the other side, the possibility (often realised) of the adoption being a commercial transaction between the parent (most frequently an unmarried mother) and a foster-parent, by which the latter receives a sum of money and takes over an unwanted child, who most frequently dies. It is horrible to contemplate.

But indeed, always, there is the dangerous position of the adopted child, who has no settled position, no legal claim on the foster-parents, who may adopt a child in the most solemn manner and keep it all through the attractive years of childhood, then, when the less attractive years of adolescence begin, or when any change in circumstances makes the adopted child no longer wanted, they can calmly withdraw their protection and turn the child out of their home. Again, I say, it is horrible to contemplate. The destiny of the adopted child is controlled throughout the unprotected years of childhood and of youth by the whim and caprice, both of the natural parent and the adopted-parent.

And do not comfort yourself by believing that these are merely imaginary troubles. They occur every day as every one knows who has any knowledge of the practice and results of child adoption in this country. I personally know of many cases of injustice that have brought disaster and unhappiness to the child. Let me tell you one. A boy was adopted by a man, unmarried, a minister of God, who was a social worker and greatly attached to children. But later in his life the man married. Under pressure from his mother, accounted as a religious and good woman, the adoption was cancelled, the boy, wanted no longer, was sent to a home for homeless children. No one troubled about him. Or take another case where an illegitimately born child—a baby girl, was abandoned and afterwards reclaimed *three times during the first five years of her life*! Each time the mother took her away from a happy home with foster-parents who loved and cared well for her. Then after a few months of neglect the mother again abandoned her. They had no legal remedy against the caprice of the mother.

These unguarded children belong to nobody. Here is an amazing gap in our law. It is worse than that—it is an amazing gap in our consciousness and sense of social responsibility. "Nobody's children!" the phrase has a pitiable and stinging significance. Yet it is just this state of things we are countenancing with our lazy and callous indifference. There are tens of thousands of little ones for whom to-day it is bitter truth that they belong to no one. Orphaned, or unwanted by their natural-parents, many of them are being adopted in the worst and most casual manner—handed out "on probation" like a cat or a dog.

And if you doubt the truth of this statement, listen to the judgment of the Committee on Child Adoption as to the disgraceful carelessness with which adoption is being carried on in this country;

> "We believe that the absence of proper control over the 'adoption' of children over seven years of age and under that age unless payment is made, results *in an undesirable traffic in child life with which no one can interfere,* unless proceedings are taken against the adopting parent for cruelty or neglect; children may be handed from one person to another, with or without payment, advertised for disposal, and even sent out of the country without any record being kept. *Intermediaries may accept children for 'adoption' and dispose of them as and when they choose.* Homes and institutions for the reception of the children exist which are not subject to any inspection."

The italics in this passage are mine; will you try to think what these conditions, *which you are permitting,* mean? Think of them with your hearts, not with your heads! And if you have a child of your own, passionately dear to your life, try to realise the abominable position—the cruelty that can hardly be escaped, as if it were *your child,* who was thus being handed callously from one person to another, without protection, without any form of legal guardianship.

We talk much of the nation's care for children. Would it not then seem a necessary step to have some just provision of our law to protect the helpless unwanted child, who at present belongs to nobody? Humanity, and even good sense answers, "Yes." The Common Law of England has hitherto always said most emphatically, "No." *Except for a reference to adoptions which has managed to slip into a marginal note of a Finance Act, there is no recognition of adoption in our laws.*

The right thing to do is the simple thing. We have on the one hand, these homeless children, whose numbers have become much larger in these last years and with the change and slackening in responsible conduct, while on the other hand, we have, an increased number of women who are childless and will never be able to marry. The problem, at its simplest, is this: What can be done to bring together the childless woman with a mother's nature and the motherless child?

I am not forgetting the Institutions that are already in existence. There are two agencies for arranging adoption, as well as other religious and social societies, and many homes, from which children can be adopted. These agencies are doing admirable work, but they cannot do a tenth part of what ought to be done. And the very worst cases, in which the child most urgently needs protection, often cannot be reached at all. This problem is too big to be muddled through privately. It is the concern of the whole nation.

The first necessary step is to legalise adoption. Until that is done, nothing can be done.

At present as I have told you, the position is one of very great danger. The law grants the foster-parents no recognised legal control over the child. The mother, or her relatives, unless obviously immoral and unfit persons, may at any time claim back the child.

Even in the most favourable circumstances there is danger, and a never-ending uncertainty that cuts at the very root of the adopted relationships. I repeat: neither the foster-parent or the child has any security. And at any time, and for any reason, the child may be taken from his home. Directly he (or she) grows up and is able to earn money, the needy relatives, with an eye on those small earnings or on the much larger sums squeezable from the foster-parents, may prove an ever-threatening nuisance. If the foster-parent acts boldly and resists such claim, the relative may apply for a writ of Habeas Corpus in the High Court, when (under the Custody of the Children's Act, 1891) the case is decided at the discretion of the Court. As a rule, the interests of the child are considered, and, in this respect, matters have much improved of late years. But even if the decision is given in favour of the foster-parents so that the child remains in the home in which it has been reared and is loved, there is a period of ceaseless anxiety; and, that the decision will be favourable is certain only when the character of the claiming relative can be proved to be bad.

So curious is the law that it is safer to adopt the child of bad or doubtful parentage (where this can be proved) than the child of good and respectable people.

The other side of the position has also to be considered. As is evident, the foster-parents may be bad. This we have seen. And what I want to emphasise further is that here too the danger threatens the unprotected child. Just as the law gives no recognised protection to the good foster-parents, so it affords no protection to the child against a bad foster-parent.

All the time I am trying to drive into your consciousness the terrible position of the child that has no legal claims; no kind of safeguard. He (or, of course, she, and the girl babies are adopted much oftener than boys) may be adopted simply as playthings, or to satisfy deeply unconscious instincts of cruelty, or as an investment for the time when they can earn money. Also they can be cast off at the caprice of their adopters.

A further and permanent injustice, operative even under happy conditions and in a good home, arises from the fact that the adopted child is without rights of inheritance. If his foster parents, however rich, die intestate, he has no share in the family property. At any time in his life he may be left penniless and friendless, without recognition that he belongs to anyone.

Such uncertainty is awful. Try to realise the suffering which it must bring to the child, ever dogging his footsteps like a menacing shadow.

Our sluggard imaginations must surely be stirred now our attention has been directed to this gap in our law. I wish that my pen had greater power to bring home to everyone concerned—and *everyone who cares or professes to care for the welfare of children is concerned*—the iniquity of allowing the continuance of conditions that must bring nothing less than tragedy into the lives of these unfortunate and unprotected little ones.

This is almost the only country which does not recognise and legalise adoption: all that needs to be done is to bring our law up to the standard which prevails in other lands. We alone are neglectful. It is one of the many social matters concerning children on which Great Britain has seriously fallen behind the example of its own daughter States. The United States, Australia and New Zealand have all gone far ahead of the Mother Country in their legislation in regard to child adoption. All the forty-eight States of the Union have now Acts regulating adoption. But perhaps the Model Act is that of Western Australia, passed in 1891. It provides for the complete and careful guardianship of all adopted children. The Act has worked admirably, and with a very few alterations could be adopted to the needs of this country.

And it must not be thought that all this recognition and protection of adoption is a new thing, and, as such, possible to dismiss as unnecessary, belonging to an over-protective and grandmotherly system of law. Such a belief would be far from the truth. Students of history know how almost universal was the practice of adoption in older civilisations. Roman law recognised the custom and adoption was extremely common. I could give many other examples. Especially interesting is the custom in India, where among the Hindoos, when a child is adopted into a new family, it goes through the religious ceremonies belonging to death before quitting the home in which it was born, and afterwards goes through the religious ceremonies belonging to birth on reaching the new home. The old bond is completely severed and a new social, religious and legal bond created.

I would ask your attention to this wise provision made by one of the oldest civilisations, which often understood so much more practically and simply the needs of a social situation.

If the full necessary security is to be given to the practice of adoption there must clearly be a complete passing over of the duties and rights of the natural-parents to the adopting parents. Adoption ought to be undertaken only solemnly and with due understanding of all the difficulties, and the necessary precautions. The closest enquiries, in every case, need to be made as to the bona fide intentions and complete suitability of the adopting parents: guarantees must be given of their intentions and ability to bring up and care for the child. It would also be equally necessary, except in exceptional cases of proved cruelty and unfit parentage, to ascertain the reasons why the parents—or parent in the case of an illegitimately born child—desired to give up their rights of guardianship. But when once this has been done, and any order of adoption made, the parental relationship ought to be transferred completely from the natural to the adopting parents.

And in the interests of the child, I would have this transference carried out with the severest restrictions. I would not allow a parent, or parents, who once gave up the guardianship of the child any rights of visitation. Such visits, even under the happiest circumstances cause disturbance, remind the child unceasingly of its difficult position as an adopted child. They tend to create confusion, with feelings of dissatisfaction and jealousy; comparison between the old home and the new home; conflicts between the affection for the adopted-parents and the very possible drawing back of natural affection for the real parents.

All ways adoption must be difficult.

Science has shewn us how terribly the future of the child depends on its early relationships in the home; its relation to its mother, on whom it depends for the first childish satisfactions, its relations to its father, to its brothers and sisters. The adopted relationships can never be quite the same as the natural relationships. We now know how easily jealousy and unhappiness can arise in the heart of even the youngest child, and what havoc to the after life these feelings may bring. If we remember this, we shall realise better the disturbing emotions likely to be aroused when one parent is lost and replaced by another. That is why everything possible needs to be done to give to adopted parenthood the strongest stability. The adoption of a child ought never to be undertaken lightly. It is, perhaps, the most binding and the most solemn, and the most fatefully responsible of any human relationship.

A righteous law of adoption needs to guard the adopted child so that the voluntary relationship is as binding in every way and as permanent as the natural relationship. For this reason the adopted child should, in my opinion, have the same rights of inheritance as all other children. Nothing short of this can do justice to the adopted child.

We talk a great deal to-day about children and their rights, but very few of us realise at all practically and fully the change of attitude, in particular in connection with property and the rights of inheritances, that are likely to be necessary, if, in all circumstances, our theories are to be expressed in our daily conduct.

The whole question is complicated and very difficult, there is, indeed, no easy way out.

LET US PENSION THE MOTHERS.

I was attending a conference to consider the best steps to be taken to aid mothers and to stop the sacrifice of the lives and health of little children. All kinds of suggestions were made. We talked much, we proposed and discussed, but none of us seemed able to agree what ought to be done.

Then a strong man, an observant lawyer, rose. He spoke with the biting American twang. His words were few: "Why don't you pay poor mothers?"

The brilliant simplicity of this question stirred at once our powers of understanding.

It was Judge Neil who spoke. In brief phrases he told us what had been done in America. Mother's pensions, which are in reality children's pensions, have been established in most of the forty-eight States of the Union. They are granted until the children are fourteen, or, in the case of delicate children, until sixteen. State-appointed supervisors watch over the welfare of the children to ensure that the money given is well spent by the mother.

As Judge Neil placed the facts before us, this plan of paying mothers instead of forcing them to go out as workers, possibly at "sweated" wages, and then paying other people in an institution to do their work, seemed so simple that I was filled with wonder that we had not long ago thought of so easy and obvious a reform. It is strange that it is so often the most simple things that we never think of doing. I believe it is because we think of reforms intellectually; we are not human enough to feel.

Now, it is just Judge Neil's humanity that set his feet upon the right way. Listen to the story of how first he came to think of mother's pensions:—

In 1911, a poor widow, broken by the burden of supporting her family, was condemned to have all her five children taken from her.

"Better to shoot her than take away her children." said Judge Neil. He then asked how much it would cost to maintain the children in a State institution.

"The country pays the institution 10 dollars a month for each child," was the answer.

"Why not give the 10 dollars to the mother and let her keep her children?"

Such was Judge Neil's humane and practical solution of the problem. Thus the scheme for pensioning mothers was born.

The responsibility of the State for children ill-cared-for is admitted in most countries. It is, therefore, a question of ways and means, not a question of high principle, how best to carry out this intention and prevent child poverty.

Surely grants to good mothers are better than grants to institutions. Even the best Poor Law schools must have the faults that are inherent in institutions.

I can hardly express too strongly my own want of faith in "expert child-trainers." I have found always that they regard the child mainly, if not entirely, as something to be improved and instructed on a definite plan. The "expert" is never human, and a child has need of all the human treatment it can get.

Every child has absolute need of its mother. All experience shows us that the home, with its sympathetic relationships of mother and child, sisters and brothers, cannot be replaced. We must insist on reforms that will make home life possible.

The child has to accept the arrangements we make; that is why this question is of such immense importance. If the matter could be fixed by the will of the children I should have no fear. The child has not lost the true values of life.

There is another fact to consider—one that will appeal to ratepayers. Grants to mothers are cheaper than grants to institutions. In the United

States the payment made to a mother works out at about one-third the cost of maintaining a child in an institution. So we can do the best thing for the child and its mother and at the same time save our pockets.

BOY AND GIRL OFFENDERS, AND ADULT MISUNDERSTANDING

Much disturbing evidence on such a grave question as the bad behaviour and consequent punishment of boys and girls, in institutions, and in prisons, is made public, from time to time, to rouse the consciousness of all those who have concern for the welfare of the young. Sometimes the events recorded are of a more serious character. The attempted suicides and continued escapes of young prisoners certainly afford a rather tragic witness of some failure in our reformative efforts. Even under the Borstal system of prison life—a system that is primarily intended to be humane and educative, and not brutal and primitive, the results obtained are far from being satisfactory. We cannot feel that we are achieving anything like what ought to be done in the difficult, but necessary, duty of reclaiming these young lives that, for one cause or another, have fallen to disaster.

If we believe, as believe we must, that the old are responsible for the young—that the one generation must stand as guardian to the next—this problem of delinquency is one that we may not thrust aside. It is bigger than its immediate application in connection with reclaiming the individual boy or the individual girl: it touches the very deepest of our duties—our duty to the future. It is for us to ask many questions of ourselves, and of all those who are in any way connected with the young; questions to which it is not easy always to find satisfactory answers.

It is obvious that something is wrong.

I do not wish to harrow you with painful statistics, or by reminding you of unfortunate incidents in connection with young prisoners that *you ought not to have forgotten. You would not have forgotten if you had cared as you ought to care.*

I do not deny that "much is being done; that conditions are better far than they were in the past." But this does not cover our failures or lessen our responsibilities. I plead for greater attention to, and more understanding of, the delinquent child. It is not, and never can be, a question that can be fixed or finally decided: the child is an individual; and, in each case, the problem of dealing with him must be a separate problem. This is certain—only by understanding the child who fails, *his own difficulties and his own failure*—can we advance. By this way only can we give aid to these young offenders, who, with a burden of ancient instincts and uncontrolled impulses, come into a world filled with undesirable examples, where they have to face manifold temptations.

Let us try, then, to consider the delinquent boy and girl, bearing these truths in our thoughts. And first we must acknowledge the complexity and terrible difficulty of the problem. Delinquency in the young cannot be explained by obvious superficial causes. The motivating impulse to naughtiness and bad conduct always lies outside of consciousness. I mean that the boy or girl who continuously does wrong, fails altogether in good conduct, whether in a reformatory, in a prison, or a Borstal institution is acting in this way from a reason which is deeply hidden, and which they do not themselves understand; while further, the present misbehaviour is connected with some experience of the past that now they have forgotten. *They are driven by this inward urge into rebellion and insubordinate conduct.* And the help they ought to have is one of re-education, by clearing up what was wrong in the past, and this help must be given to them by those who are specially trained to understand.

They cannot, unaided, help themselves. The things they do wrong—the breaking of rules, the failures in work, the violent conduct, the attempted escapes—in the vast majority of cases, are a defence against unhappiness that stalks as a deadly shadow, following their young lives.

Their treatment is a medical as well as a social and ethical problem. The young do wrong because their souls are sick. Such a statement is not fantastic, it is seriously true. To understand the meaning of the present bad conduct of anyone, but especially of the delinquent boy or girl, it is absolutely necessary to find out the motive which makes them want to behave badly. Always we have to search to find "a reason why." To discover, as far as we are able, what it is causing the rebellion or the bad conduct, we must have wisdom to give up the old ignorant ideas as to its being possible to cure bad conduct, in any way that matters, by scoldings, by punishments or, indeed, any kind of direct attack.

The fault that distresses those in authority in the present must be regarded as the sign of a hidden conflict that has distressed the child in the past. It is this conflict, then, that must be discovered and dealt with. Never in any case can the lazy adult view be accepted that the delinquent child does wrong because of original sin.

The young do wrong when they suffer, usually through the blunders of those who are supposed to train them; their faults in behaviour are a relief for pain they find too intolerable to bear. If the boy or girl is happy in harmony with his or her world, then that boy or girl is good.

To find the real cure for this unhappiness of soul is, of course, a most difficult task. It can be accomplished completely only by those specially trained in understanding and analysing the child mind. But much good, and a return to healthy happiness can often be gained, by a little helpful understanding of the special problems of the individual boy or girl. It is the educator's duty to try to pour daylight on the hidden plague spots of the soul.

This can never be done by cruelty or any form of coercive treatment which arouses fear—the most deadly enemy to right conduct. The way to educate the abnormal, the difficult boy or girl, is not to be shocked or to punish them, but to show them sympathy, directed by knowledge.

Teach these girls and boys that they have failed in good conduct, not because they are bad or different really from other more fortunate young people, but because they have been unhappy—ill with feelings of insecurity, of deficiency, of loneliness, of failure; help them to understand the causes that have brought about this condition, why they have felt inferior, been unhappy; and then build up their characters by giving them new opportunities of finding happiness in their work and in their play, providing new interests and creating opportunities for new responsibilities. These young people want kindness and to be taught to be sociable. Moral conduct is never easy. We all want what we do want. We surrender our wishes only because we find we satisfy other desires by so doing. We are praised and rewarded for good conduct and for preferring to give up to others what we want to do ourselves. And a very practical lesson in our training of delinquents depends upon this. The educators must take the greatest possible care that bad conduct does not give greater pleasure than good conduct. Doing wrong so often opens for the young the widest and easiest door to gain excitement. If boys and girls in Borstal institutions and in reformatories are left unnoticed and never praised when good they quickly feel neglected. And though they do not recognise these disappointed feelings they act very strongly in setting them to seek for some kind of relief. And if allowed to enjoy power when they become rebellious, through the notice that is bestowed upon them and the upsetting of the usual regime of the school or the prison workshop, they will continue to indulge in bad conduct whenever they are bored or, for any reason, crave some form of emotional relief.

Bad conduct is primitive, infantile conduct, and one of its strongest characteristics is the tendency to proceed more directly, more unthinkingly, and more selfishly to the goal of the wishes than is usually done by the reasonable adult.

The little child wants something, grabs at it, and when it does not at once get it, screams and breaks into a passion.

Now this is just what is done by the delinquent boy or girl, whose conduct must be regarded as infantile, frankly selfish, and regulated only by doing what one wants and getting what one wants. Such conduct points to a condition of retarded growth; and usually can be traced back to some mistake in the early training, which has prevented an adaptation of the character to grown-up conditions, so that the boy or girl of seventeen or eighteen acts still like the young child of four or five years of age.

Every child, who is to grow into a successful and happy adult, has to grow out of this primitive behaviour and to learn social standards of conduct—to think what other people want and to measure their own conduct in its relation to others.

Thus the real problem of the education of the delinquent boy or girl is to help them to grow up. And the very first step is to teach them to stop thinking about themselves. They have to learn to turn outwards towards others and away from their own wishes and hidden desires, that are the real cause of their unhappiness and bad conduct.

And for this reason, even if for no other, there could be no possible form of treatment as harmful, and also I may add so silly, as that adopted (as still so often it is) in reformatory institutions of placing insubordinate prisoners in solitary confinement, even sometimes with the use of irons. No other form of punishment could be more disastrous to a boy or girl. To permit this cruelty is assuredly to increase the faults of character that are the cause of the bad conduct. By such insane punishment the young offenders are separated from their companions, perhaps bound, and left without occupation to sit alone, brooding over their unhappiness; their thoughts necessarily fixed upon themselves. They cannot fail by means of this unhealthy process to be sent more backwards into childish and bad behaviour—driven further away from adult and social conduct.

Few of us, I think, understand sufficiently how continuous and almost unspeakably hard, are the efforts that the delinquent has to make in order to achieve re-education. He is overwhelmingly conscious (however much he may seem to be indifferent) of his own inferiority. All such boys or girls, who frequently become aggressive and insubordinate, need to be treated in such a way as will increase their confidence in themselves. This may seem contradictory, but it is true. If the young offenders are punished and discouraged the trouble from which they suffer is sure to increase by making stronger the sense of self-depreciation. Too often the devastating feelings are driven back into the obscure places of the mind—the unseen office of the directing forces that in secret issue the supreme commands that control conduct. It is in order the better to overcome the truths that would stab him about himself if he recognised them, that such a wrong-doer becomes aggressively self-assertive, indulges in foolish acts and marked insubordination. Such boys and girls are without courage, and all their pride boils up behind a maimed and timid character.

The important thing to remember is that, though bad conduct comes from what seems insubordination, "the characteristics of bad conduct" arise from the state of the boy's or girl's mind, and that state depends very much on the treatment he (or she) receives.

If you cure the particular fault for which the punishment was inflicted, and the boy or girl loses his (or her) soul, you have done more harm than good. But the real position is worse than that, for if you hurt the young soul, you give up for ever the opportunity of re-educating the boy or girl for good conduct.

NEW WAYS OF TEACHING CHILDREN

UNBOUNDED FREEDOM AND SOME DRAWBACKS

I remember once seeing in "Punch" a picture that has always retained in my memory the vividness of the first impression. It is a long time ago, yet I can see it now exactly as I saw it then. A father, at a children's Christmas party, was personating a bear. Filled with the adult's joy of being allowed to be a child, he was roaring loudly, as he crawled upon the floor covered with a woolly hearth-rug. So much for the father. Certainly he was enjoying it. But what about the children. What was their view of this performance?

They were all looking bored. Even the tiny ones shewed no enthusiasm. In the corner of the room as far withdraw as space permitted was a group of young school boys, very stiffly correct in Etons and immense white collars. They were disgusted. One, who had ostentatiously turned his back on the performing father, was plainly angry. Even his back was eloquent of disapproval and gloom surrounded him. His companion, standing next to him, attempted to cheer him in this way: "Never mind, Brown major, you know its not *your* fault if your pater is a blooming fool!"

It is, indeed, a different aspect of the situation. The son ashamed of the father! The young generation condemning the old! It is fitting that we should take notice and remember the lesson that is taught.

For this picture of appraising youth carries a very real moral that should be considered by those modern educational enthusiasts, who are always talking about amusing the child—as if that were the one thing which mattered. There is no subject, I believe, on which greater nonsense is talked than on this one of interesting children. Personally I am sceptical whether children are ever greatly interested in the entertainments that the adult provides for their amusement. What they find interesting are the things they provide for themselves. That is one reason why there must be so great an element of falsity in modern educational theories, which aim at making lessons so interesting that they become like play.

It cannot be done.

Much of this kind of talk sounds admirable from the point of view of the adult, but what I always want to know is the view taken by the child—by the boy or the girl. I do not think they are quite *so fond of being amused* as we are apt to believe. Nor do I think they can be, or indeed, ought to be, *interested* (which is the same really as being amused) *to adult orders*. I *mean* that to be truly effective and liberating to the child, this interest must be dependent on what he has to do for himself. The work cannot be done for him. That is why I am afraid of the incursion into the schoolroom of the too anxious and amusement-providing spirit of the home. It causes too much indirect interference. It supplies too many appliances. It is over-occupied with arrangements and the smoothing away of difficulties. In a word it does not leave the child sufficiently to himself to learn his own lessons, to satisfy his own needs in his own way.

It proposes, of course, to do this, but it is just here that enormous mistakes occur.

I can fancy a group of boys and girls who, if they said what they really felt about their own education and our ceaseless experiments and efforts to make their lessons interesting and more acceptable to them, would pity us as fools.

The point of view of the child (also of the boy and the girl, but especially, I think, of the boy) is always so utterly different from the point of view of the adult. You see they are judging the situation personally, while we are judging it vicariously and ethically.

The ever-pressing idea of the educationalist to-day is to give the child freedom. But what is freedom? That is a question to which we have not yet found an answer. Do we consider sufficiently, if what means freedom to us, really gives freedom to the young? And a second question—Are we not, perhaps, in our nervous over-anxiety, imposing upon them something they do not want?

There is a great deal said about self-development and the necessity of the teacher respecting the child's individuality. We are continually hearing of interesting experiments made in free schools and are told of children who, even when quite young, if left to choose their own tasks, will be so interested in writing, in reading, and also in arithmetic, that they will not want to give up their work even when school-hours are over!

Still I am unconvinced. I would rather have the boy or the girl waiting in eagerness for the bell to ring to free them from the school.

We are apt to over-estimate our grown-up power. We do this because we like to do it. It flatters adult egotism. We find a delicious sense of power in realising ourselves in so many new ways as potters to mould the clay of the child's mind. I often feel that we worry about this question of education much more to please ourselves than to help the young.

But this continuous occupation with the child is bad for the child, however gratifying it is to ourselves. By the provision of too many appliances and "helps to learn," and by continual experiments that are too often changed, we tend to check creative originality, and thereby we destroy the interest we are labouring to stimulate. It is better for the child if we are less occupied with his needs. If we do not provide him with interests he will find them for himself. In this case they will mean more to him—do more for him. I dislike exceedingly all contrivances that make things easy. I believe the child dislikes them too. That is one reason why he tires so soon of all the appliances you provide. They do not stimulate interest and effort, except quite temporarily, indeed, they destroy both.

This applies to children's play quite as much as to their schoolwork. Most children to-day are given too many and too elaborate toys. Perhaps nothing is more mentally destructive. The child will invent his own amusements. He wants to fight giant lamp-posts and to go to sea in an inverted table. To fasten his imagination to your adult suggestions is to destroy his vigour.

Know then this truth. You can teach the child lessons and you can discipline him by your grown up authority, *but you cannot by your ready-made devices successfully interest him or give him freedom*. That he must find for himself. He cannot develop fully and be reliant, unless by himself, and very often *against your will*, he travels on his own road.

There is the very greatest delusion about this idea of freedom in the school room. And it is open to question whether the children in the free school, left mainly to choose their own tasks and take their own time in performing them, are really freer, in any true sense, than the disciplined and directed children in the master-ruled schools who have, in my experience, much better opportunities in the out-of-school hours of developing personality. The discipline of the school does help them by giving them more rest. I think they are less influenced by their teacher. For always there is, and must be, whatever the educational plan and however free from apparent compulsions, behind the pupil the will of the teacher indirectly, if not directly, guiding. And I am not sure if this indirect coercion of suggestion is not worse, from the point of view of the child, than the old-fashioned methods of direct command. I will even go further and state my belief that its claims are heavier, and bind the boy or girl more permanently in the prison of obedience.

For one thing, such indirect coercion does close for the pupils the splendid liberating door of being rebellious.

I can still remember the excitement and real health-giving joy I obtained when, as a child, I once out-witted my instructor and escaped from my lessons, which I heartily detested, to go to a fair we had all been forbidden to visit. There was a glorious fat woman, and a man who swallowed swords! Wonderful! And there was a delicious sweet in a long roll of twisted pink and white, with inside a picture of Roger, the Claimant. It was the time of the Tichbourne trial. If you could find one tiny piece of the sweet without the picture, a whole immense bar, much bigger than those which were ordinarily sold, was to be forfeited and given to you free! Think of it! The possibility! The excitement! Every penny I had was spent—and it was worth it! Yes, a thousand times worth it! Of course, what I did brought punishment. For I had to confess my misdeeds. Those sweets made me very sick. What did that matter? I did gain the joy and liberty I was seeking. This was one of the really educating experiences of my childhood.

Seriously, I am deeply afraid that to-day in our very eagerness to help children, we may often be acting in an exactly opposite direction as a hinderance to their self-development, and future happiness. I believe we are trying to achieve something that is impossible.

One thing I am certain we ought to accept. It is the inescapable barrier between the generations—between the parents and the children, the teachers and the pupils. The young ought to be separated from the old. I think this biological fact is forgotten by many advocates of freedom and new ideals in education.

I believe also that the young want—and by "want" I mean both desire and need—the direction of the old. They want the authority that marks the division between the two generations, for this opens up opportunities to rebel. Instinctively they know they can find more liberty under authority, than when left with the pressing burden, often too heavy for their young inexperience, of deciding at school, as well as at home, almost everything for themselves.

Nor do I very much believe in the over-worrying conscientiousness of the modern teachers. Again I must insist upon this. The increasing preoccupation with the child; the constant trying of different educational experiments, is almost certain to exercise an adverse influence. There may be a tyranny of solicitude and kindness that is harder to bear than scoldings and punishments. To me there is something mournful in this chorus of uncertainty, in which it is not difficult to detect the poverty of our faith. It tells a tale of infirmity both of life and purpose. So small a thing staggers us. We are without confidence in ourselves or in life. Why is this?

Do we, I often ask myself, know at all, what the child wants to find the freedom that gives liberty to the young soul—the only freedom that matters? How can we give the gifts of life unless we have ourselves firmer confidence? If anything can destroy the soul of a child, it is want of security. Our irresolution is our great danger. That is why so often our efforts are barren. It is a sign of a nervous disorder of the soul. We seek to gain from outside things what we should find within ourselves. And the child must suffer. For the child is so helplessly dependent, so inarticulate, so unable to express his own feelings and deeper needs.

There is still the most amazing blindness in regard to the effect of adult conduct on the child. I know of one small boy who was taught in a free school, where the idea of authority was held in abhorrence. Yet this boy of eight was found one night sobbing bitterly. His mother questioned him. It appeared he had been idle at school, rude, and generally naughty. He had not been scolded, and, of course, not punished. He had been reasoned with and told the foolishness of behaving in this way. Apparently all ought to have been well. Yet it was just in this reasonable gentleness of his headmaster that his trouble rested. He knew he had been naughty. He *wanted* the punishment that would have wiped out his own consciousness of wrong doing. He sobbed out his complaint to his mother, "if only he (his teacher) had punished me or been cross and nasty I could have forgotten. It would have been all over. But now I keep on thinking about it, and I feel *all twisted up inside.*"

Now this young boy understood his own needs much better than did his master, who was making the very common mistake of judging the child by himself. The needs of the child are entirely different from the needs of the adult. The child wants security, he wants firmness, he desires authority, he even wants punishment.

Let me tell you another story to help to bring home these forgotten truths. This time it was a little girl of the tender age of six years, who had done wrong, was rude and very unkind to her governess. The occasion was a birthday party. Over-excitement was the outside cause of her bad behaviour. No one minded the rude remarks except the child herself. We all, including the insulted governess, understood the reason. Our mistake was, we understood too well, or rather, we judged from the outside and from our grown-up point of view, forgetting that it was not that of the child. We all tried to comfort the little one's distress, assuring her we understood and knew she did not mean what she had said. In vain. The child would not be comforted. I can never forget the fatalism of her remark, "It does not matter that Miss —— and all of you forgive me, what matters is that I *did* it."

Again it was the child, not we—the grown-ups, who understood the situation as it really was. And what I want to impress upon you, is the suffering unwittingly imposed on both these children. If they had been punished they would not have felt this paralysing sense of wrong doing—a suffering of the soul, fitting perhaps for the adult, but not for the child. With punishment or even with scolding, the penalty would have been paid, and the relief would have been gained of self-forgiveness—a relief so much more necessary to happiness than the forgiveness of others.

Of course, it may be argued that morally such self-accusation which does follow from this method of adult forgiveness, with its sentimental treatment of wrong doing, is good for children. I do not think so. Certainly it makes them suffer—suffer intolerably and to an extent that few adults are sufficiently discerning to realise. But the burden placed on the untried, unhardened and sensitive child-soul is, I am certain, too heavy for them to bear safely at this stage of their psychic growth. Punishment would, in almost all cases, be far easier and more acceptable. It would also be far healthier. There is always the gravest danger in placing the immature child in any position that forces an emotional response in advance of the stage of development which has been reached. We have to see these problems as the child feels them, not as we think about them with our grown-up experience and adult deadness.

DIFFICULTIES AND MISTAKES IN SEX EDUCATION

To the theoretical teacher or parent eager to reform the world on paper, it may seem easy to introduce sex education into the nursery training of the home, and into the curriculum of our schools. It appears a comparatively easy matter to tell the little child the truth about its own body, and as it grows older, to give carefully prepared lessons about plants and animals, which shall lead it slowly and beautifully into the way of knowledge.

Text books have been written, pamphlets officially issued, schemes drawn up for home and school instruction, and rules laid down—new finger-posts to right conduct, whereby the younger generation may be enlightened and (as we hope) by this means saved from making the mistakes that we ourselves have made.

I wish it were as simple as this. That sex instruction could be taken from books.

Of late various attempts have been made to focus attention on this aspect of the question or on that; we have been told how this teaching should be given, and with still greater assurance how it should not be given; this must be done and that must not be done; this said and that left unsaid. And groups of earnest-minded parents and teachers, in almost every town, have met together to discuss and decide debatable points; lecturers have been applied for, and their utterances have been listened to as a new gospel; yet I venture to think that, as in all other experimental and debatable questions, the very multitude of counsel and the earnestness that is expended, indicates the uncertainty of our knowledge and the doubtful value of many of our affirmations.

I find a tendency amongst most grown-ups, and especially teachers and advanced parents who ought to know better, to place too firm a reliance on their own power to educate the young in sex. I myself have done this. Like those drowning in deep water where they cannot swim, we have clutched at any plank of hope. You see so many of the old planks—religion, social barriers, chaperones, home restrictions, and so many more, on which our parents used to rely, have failed us; been broken in our hands by the vigorous destroying grasp of the young generation; and, therefore, we have clutched with frantic fingers at this new fair-looking life-raft, in pursuit of the one aim, to protect our children.

But will it save them? I doubt if it will except in a limited and very different way from what is usually accepted. We cannot help the young very far or deeply by any of our teaching. Not only do they want their own experience, not ours, but it is right for them to have it. The urge of adolescence carries them away out of our detaining hands. And I think it may be well that at once we realize and acknowledge the very narrow limits of our power.

Thus I have nothing new or very striking to bring to the solution of this difficult problem. I shall endeavour, however, to look at the matter broadly and practically, and attempt to indicate in what direction, as it seems to me, further progress may be made at the present stage of our very faulty knowledge.

One of the most disturbing features that we have to recognise in relation to the child is the very early age at which sex manifests itself. It was formerly supposed that the sex-life began at the age of puberty. Nothing is more untrue. Every child is born with instincts and desires—feelings of love, of hate, of jealousy, which furnish the motives of conduct, and are accompanied by physical manifestations of pleasure or discomfort which express themselves, often in a veiled way, as wishes and cravings, that find relief in action, and must therefore be yoked either to some burden of utility or to some car of vanity.

It should be noted, however, that the word sexual is somewhat ambiguous, because I want to stretch it to include the very germs that afterwards blossom into the adult sex-life. The little girl with her doll is maternal, and the boy with a tin sword is showing the crudest manifestation of the male protective instinct.

The baby whenever it enjoys the satisfaction of realising its infantile wants gurgles with delight. "Every nurse, and every mother who tends her child herself knows this, and recognises as a necessary task in the training of the child, almost from the day of its birth, the winning of it away from this egocentric concentration on its own body." 2

We are always trying not to admit that we have to recognise in relation to sex the very early age at which it manifests itself. We do not believe this, because we dislike to believe it. Our fear causes us to neglect in a quite wrong way the deeply affective results of the early childish emotions.

To the uninstructed eye, early desires and feelings connected with sex are often so unlike their final form that they pass unrecognised. But the mother who has eyes to see and knowledge to understand knows that the child can hide no secret. When the lips speak not, the faces in twitching mouth and blinking eyes; the hands, in telling gestures; the biting nails; the sucking thumb; the shuffling feet; the toes that are played with and sucked—all these utter the truth; and betrayal escapes out of every nervous movement of hands, and feet, and face.

We will not see and acknowledge the presence of these early emotions because we want to see the child an angel. We cannot surrender the picture of childhood as a period of delightful ignorance and innocence.

The very reverse is the truth. The child has brought with it much from more primitive times; just in the same way as its body still shows traces of earlier developments in life, so its emotions, its instincts, its wishes and desires, revert back, in many particulars, to lower stages of growth. Always the child has to fight its way upwards, and indeed, it has no easy task to find and keep the right path, in its short journey of discovery to reach from the savagery of the babe to the level of a civilised social man or woman. If we do not help it, the way becomes doubly hard and often the path is lost or, in other words, the savage triumphs.

We are now in a better position to answer the question, so much debated, as to the age at which the sex education of the child should begin. Instead of this being a matter that can be put off until the child is older, and the angel innocence has been sullied by contact with an evil and ugly world, it becomes overwhelmingly important that *no time whatever should be lost*. Every effort must be made to educate from the very hour of birth these primitive instincts, which, though permissible in the savage and the little child, are wholly wrong if allowed to remain active in the later adult years. Delay is fatal. Time lost now never can be regained: mistakes made cannot be put right. A wrong direction may most easily be given by a careless act. I cannot emphasise this too strongly, or too often. *The character, the life history and the entire fate of every child is fixed in the nursery.*

The mistake we have been making for so long is in regarding this instruction in sex as something we can impart to children or with-hold from them; a subject we may teach or not teach; enlightenment we may give to them or conceal from them. This view is entirely erroneous. In one sense, the whole matter really lies outside of our wills. Sex education cannot be omitted by any parent or any teacher from the training of any child, for it is given *by not being given*, just as surely as the other way about. There is no escape for anyone who has to do with a child.

You will see what I mean. It is not the good and wise lessons you may give, of nicely arranged explanations, with flower illustrations or stories of the mating of birds and animals; still less is it warnings or goody-goody talks about purity; nor is it any kind of formal or even conscious instruction that will have the true moulding influence on the character and emotional state of the child; but what most influences him, or in other words, teaches him, and helps or hinders him, is the peculiarly affective state—I mean, the emotional attitude—which usually is totally unknown to the parents and educators, and is also quite incomprehensible to the child himself. It is all the things that the grown-ups are trying hardest to hide from the children and perhaps also covering away from themselves that are the real directing forces in their character. The concealed enmity, or even small disharmonies between the parents, the repressed tempers, the strangled temptations, the secret longing of one or other parent, the miseries that are hidden—all these inevitably arouse a response in the children, which acting continuously and unconsciously bring them to a state corresponding with that of the parents. Their shame and want of joy in sex will become the children's shame and want of joy; their unhappiness in love will be the children's unhappiness;

their most hidden wishes will escape to create disharmonies in these young and tender souls.

The parents, and especially the mother, impress deeply into the child's being the seal of their characters, and the more sensitive and mouldable the child the deeper is the impression. Take, for instance, the only or favourite child, who suffers under an anxious excess of tenderness, so that his love is so fixed on the mother, that not only does he become restless with too heavy a burden of emotional stress, and often really ill, but in later life he has the greatest difficulty in establishing his own character, freeing himself from the mother's influence, or finding his own love-mate. Again, in the exact opposite position, there is the neglected and unwanted child, who, missing his rightful possession of love, suffers from a sense of inferiority, which dark and hindering shadow dogs his footsteps through life, finding a positive expression in shyness and incapacity for action, or a negative expression in bombastic and disagreeable self-assertion. So I might continue with countless examples. Adult traits can, in almost all cases, be traced back to the child's early experiences in connection with its parents and in its home.

The child is like a flower, and the banks where it grows are its world—its home and the friends with whom it comes in contact; the sky above is the surrounding love on which it is dependent, and to which it looks up as the flower to the sun for gladness and for life. What I mean is this: the child has desires and impulses of its own, but it reflects the changing needs and atmosphere of the small world in which it lives, and is terribly dependent on that world. It is forming and selecting a character. It very largely tries what the effect is of different kinds of conduct—different characters. The child does not itself know what it is or would wish to be. Whenever there is, as often there must be, a mistake made, a wrong step taken—a conflict inevitably occurs, and must find some quick response in childish naughtiness; otherwise dullness and unhappiness will arise; and this, if continued, will tend to bring the dangerous condition of the repressed and introverted child.

We have established now that the love-life of the child starts at a very early age; it begins in the home, and I want to investigate this love-life. To do this we must examine with some care the child's emotional relationships to the members of his family.

These relationships are not as amicable or peaceful as at first sight would appear. At a very early age jealousy as well as love stirs in the baby's soul. This may surprise you. But I would ask you for a moment to consider the baby's position. The child is in a small shut-up world with its mother. At first she occupies all its life. She is the earliest love object and of supreme importance in the infantile constellation. Everything starts from her. She is the source of nutrition and as such the first object towards which the hunger-wish is directed. She is also the supplier of warmth, of comfort, of rest—the personification of shelter and happiness—the starting point of all those interests of the child which lie outside its own body. Who can wonder at the child's possessive feelings in relation to its mother. But we have seen already, in an earlier essay, how the superfluous father comes as an intruder into this mother-child circle. And it is in this way jealousy begins to awaken, at a very early age, and sometimes is almost unbelievably active in the baby soul. For these feelings will increase if the baby is a boy, and the love of the mother may grow to great intensity, which coupled with the jealousy of the father may work great evil, especially if the mother is unwise, too tenderly solicitous, too possessive in her love, herself neurotic. In the case of the girl the position is different. The baby fixation upon the mother is, as a rule, relieved with growth, as a part of the love-fund is transferred to the father. Sometimes this does not happen, especially when the jealousy of the little girl is roused, usually by a brother or sister more loved by the mother than herself. Then, indeed, a fixation happens, either in a too passionate tenderness for the mother, which, persisting acts as an insurmountable hindrance in the later life in preventing the normal out-going of love to a member of the opposite sex. I know of one such case and it may make my meaning plainer if I tell it to you. A little girl was born in a home where there was already a brother, passionately loved by a too good mother. The little girl soon felt, for no one feels so quickly as a little child, that the brother had a place of greater importance than herself. She did not hate outwardly this brother, had she done this all might have been well, as she would have gained relief in expression. She developed the usual device of the unhappily jealous child and took to phantasy making—pretending that she had another mother, or, at other times, that she was doing some wonderful deed, being very clever, very good, very beautiful, so as to gain the love and admiration of her mother. This was the inner life of make-believe. The outer life was one of continuous nervous trouble, which culminated in St. Vitus's Dance. What is, however most interesting, is the later love-life and the startling way it reflects this early emotional conflict. This child is now a woman nearing thirty, very charming, very nice-looking; but she is utterly unable to settle on her love-mate. Engagement has followed engagement, in each case the lover has been discarded for no adequate reason. In all other connections of life capable and good, she behaves in her love affairs with a capricious unkindness, very difficult to pardon if one did not understand.

It may be worth while to refer to another case known to me. Two daughters, with a mother and father between whom there was trouble, the father having an affection for another woman. Though the trouble was most carefully hidden from the little girls it formed the decisive factor in their lives. It is not clear to me whether the love-object was the father, though I think that this was so. It was, however, the mother who was, as, indeed, usually she is, the central figure in this nursery drama. Both children suffered jealousy, probably of the lady loved by the father, transferred to the mother. The effect was directly opposite on each daughter. The elder, stronger and more forceful charactered girl developed a passionate rebellion against the mother, a specially sweet and long-suffering woman, of so violent and unreasonable character that she could not live at home; while the other child was the absolute type of the perfect daughter, self-sacrificing and passionately loving. But why this case is interesting is that it was the good child who suffered while the bad child triumphed. The rebellious daughter was able to establish her own adult life, to work successfully and to marry happily; the dutiful daughter lost her own power to live and to love, and was not liberated even by the death of the mother. I would ask you to note this very specially as it is exceedingly important. A too great devotion and anxious excess of tenderness on the part of any one, but especially on the part of a child to a parent, covers always, and even under the most improbable circumstances, as when it appears that there is the closest sympathy and harmony of will, an intense hostile tendency. And because vice will not be choked by virtue, this over submissive state is much more dangerous and likely to destroy the springs of life than open hostility.

We have much less need to be afraid of the future for the rebellious, even the unkind and ungrateful child, than for the good and devoted child who apparently knows no will but ours, and lives in outward perfect submission. Every parent who is wise will recognise such a state as one of the greatest danger, and at any cost to herself will separate herself from the child. Mind, I do not mean send the child away. That plan may, indeed, be tried, but often, especially with sensitive children, the absence will but forge the fetters firmer. Something like this happens whenever a child who goes to school, is continuously homesick and becomes ill, not necessarily with a specified illness, but grows nervous, fails in work and in play. Such a mother has before her, perhaps the hardest task in parenthood. She has to take the child home and dissipate and send from herself the over-tender love, accepting in its place the rebellious hatred that it covers. Does she fail in this task of sacrifice, made necessary, remember, by some early mistake in the management of the child, she is simply using up for herself the energy of love, which her child ought to have to use for its own life.

I trust these two cases will have made plainer to you the kind of difficult problems that have to be met by parents. I do not think there is any family where they are not present. There are many variations, and the strength of the difficulty as well as the permanent nature of the harm suffered by the child, depends almost wholly on the wisdom and the knowledge of the mother, and, even more, on the extent to which she has been able to understand her concealed wishes and her own love-history from her childhood's days and free herself from its heritage. You will see, I think, without my waiting to point out how complex the position is, and how hard is the task of the mother to guide the early emotional life of her children. It is obvious how easily mistakes may be made.

Hardly less difficult is the position of the father, who is at once the intruder in the family and the supporter of it. To the child, in the ordinary home, he is the final authority. He occupies the position of a god or a ruler. He is feared and rebelled against, also he is reverenced. Any omission of these qualities, and especially the last, is fatal to the child. Without this father reverence, and in absence of his needed authority, there arises an arrogant disposition that controls all the later character. As has been recognised by all modern psychologists, there is much of the childish attitude of the boy to his father in the later relations of the follower to his ruler, of the worshipper to his god, of the schoolboy to his school-master.

Every boy looks forward to the day when he can escape the rule of the father and himself usurp his power. I think you will find here the secret spring of all later rebellion against authority, either in the boy or in the man. I must give another warning. Again, it is when these childish feelings of rebellion, jealousy and hate are hidden, and work in the child's soul without his knowledge, that the greatest harm is done.

In this connection, I may recount the case of a boy who grew out of babyhood shewing unusual affection for his step-father. He was also too much attached to his mother—being in that most unfortunate position of an only and too-much-considered child—and in consequence suffered from strongly jealous feelings towards the step-father. In this way a conflict was aroused between love and hate, and serious nervous symptoms arose. The origin of the trouble was first discovered at about ten years, when the boy developed a very passionate hatred against God. He was overheard one day swearing on his toy sword to devote his life to killing God. As he had not been brought up in an over-religious home, and had hardly ever been taken to Church, this vehement hatred, which continued for some time, was noticed as unusual. Now the specialist consulted about the nervous symptoms at once found in this God-hatred a projection of the very common boyish hatred to the father. The parents learnt that this was a sign of health, an effort the boy was making to rid himself of an unbearable inward trouble.

I would emphasise the necessity of parents having the right knowledge and the love that will enable them to recognise what is important in the development of character. Too little attention is given by parents to the spontaneous utterances of children: it is these that will give the clue to what is troubling the child. Questions never get direct and real answers. It is what the child brings out unconsciously that should be noted; his wishes hidden, as a rule, under some symbol, that the parent unaided, may find very difficult to interpret. We are too apt—and in this mothers are the worst sinners—to consider their children as unthinking beings. Always, I believe, children know more than we credit to them. This is true, in particular, of all emotional states. As I have tried to make plain, it is these emotions acting and interacting in connection with the home relations which are of lasting importance. Mothers who even in the nursery overforce the emotional growth of their little ones, with the unceasing demands of an over-demonstrative and unhealthy tenderness; fathers, who, themselves too arrogant for power, allow their boys and girls no independent possession of their own lives—such parents are the destroyers of their children. Their thoughtlessness and ignorance create problems that are tragedies of pain to children, and leave them marred, and often maimed, for their conflict with life.

I am prepared for an objection. You may some of you be thinking that this picture I have drawn for you of nursery tragedies is coloured from my imagination and without sufficient relation to truth. "Little children," you may be saying, "cannot feel these devastating adult passions. You are projecting on to them evils created by your own diseased mind." And you turn back to your "angel innocence" belief, which must be true, at any rate, you are convinced in the case of your own child.

But may I tell you this: you must not come to these problems of the child with an already fixed conviction that they do not exist; because this may well be, not because they are not there—active even in your own nursery—but because you shut your eyes determined not to see them. You think this about their not being present, because you want to think it, not because it is true. Also it is very easy even for the wisest parent to be led astray; for the child is the most accomplished actor, and is always hiding its real self from you.

You see the child has truly a very hard part to play, a part it can lay down only when no grown-ups are by. In surroundings very opposed to its own desires or its primitive needs, while still a savage in emotions, it has to pretend to be what you think it is, to do what you think it ought to do, and like what you think it ought to like. It has filled me often with wonder and admiration to see the really brilliant way in which even the youngest children play up to the angel-role forced upon them by grown-ups. Much naughtiness and many violent unexplained tempers are really a breakdown in this part. The right cue is forgotten at the right moment, or the correct entrance is missed. And I feel it very necessary to emphasise to you that the naughty child is not so much being naughty as being himself. He rushes at you with a knife, not because he is in a temper, but rather the temper is the liberating key which allows his real desire to kill you to break through the barricade of civilised desires that you are building around him. And it is very necessary for the grown-up to understand the intense satisfaction of creative strength which the child gains by this breaking out of his real self—a satisfaction that is greatly marred, it is true, and even turned to pain, by the consciousness of knowing he has broken adult rules of behaviour, been a naughty boy and grieved you. Always there is this conflict going on between his primitive egocentric desires and the demands of the adult world in which he has to learn to live. It is this conflict, and his success and failure in it, which determines his growth. More and more he has to learn to give up his own desires and subordinate his own will. Yet, I am not sure if his repentence, when he fails, is altogether good for him. Certainly, if it is excessive, and if it occurs too frequently, it weakens the force of life. And it is most urgent of all to remember that the parent, or nurse, or teacher, by constantly requiring from the uncivilised child the standard of conduct right for the civilised adult may, and most frequently does, produce a strain which turns the creative force of life back upon itself. It is ever thus in life when we draw back too hastily or too much coerced, from any spontaneous expression of emotion; the energy gathered for the direct expression flows back impotent. I believe that many a creative artist is destroyed in the civilising process of the child being turned into the good boy or girl.

And this brings me to a question of the most urgent importance to all parents and teachers who attempt to guide the emotional development of a child; to go slowly, and never to force an outward practice of virtue from the child, if that particular stage of virtue has not been reached. We do not expect the child to read until it has learnt to read, nor to calculate and work sums before it understands the use of figures; we do not expect it to walk until it has stumbled and fallen many times, nor to use its tiny hands with precision until it has broken many objects. Why then should we expect it to be good without learning to be good? And especially, I ask, why should we demand a standard of emotional behaviour much in advance of anything to which we ourselves have attained?

For in truth every child has a twisted and most difficult path to travel in order to reach the standard of conduct expected by the adult world. Few parents realise at all the harm that so readily may be done, from any over-hastening on the road to virtue, to the child, sensitive, responsive to every suggestion, most liable to injury; who is always balanced between the desire to be a dirty, little savage, like himself, or a clean well-behaved person, like a grown-up. For what gives every adult so tremendous a hold over the child is his never ceasing desire to push forward to a stage above what he is at. Always he is pulled in two directions, forward to effort and good conduct and the real world of action and of grown-ups, and backward towards ease and self-pleasing and the dream-world of the child, in which he thinks only of what he wants himself. If we hurry him too much there will be a regression: the uncivilised trait that has not been got rid of by experience of its uselessness and voluntarily been cast aside, will be thrust down deep into the psyche, where its unrealised power sends up primitive and uncivilised wishes, which will certainly mar the adult life, even if they do not wreck it.

It is not from sheer "contrariness" or "nastiness" that children develop "bad habits," that they pick noses, bite nails, stammer, and other much worse things, or later are too shy or too boisterously self-assertive, or develop illness and morbid fears. [3] Such symptoms may be replacements of infantile curiosities and interests which were denied their satisfaction by the mother's warning, often harmful, however gently given, "that is not nice, darling." In particular harm is caused by a too early checking of the child's delight in messy things, making mud pies, playing with water, using hands instead of knife and fork, and other nasty messy habits. The particular habit may, and usually does, disappear, but the checked and thwarted energy is still potent and at any time in after life may re-appear clothed in a fresh dress of concealment.

All that can be done with the bad habit is to turn it into new directions of rightful energy. As, for instance, the messy child should be given heaps of plasticine or wax, and sand to play with. Similarly with the desire to play with water: this is a symbolic action by which the young child frees itself from some inner hidden trouble. I know of one case where a child until quite an advanced age, always after a relapse into bad and primitive behaviour, had a curious way of blowing water through long tubes. The result was highly satisfactory and never failed to bring the child back to good and social behaviour. As an example of the terrible harm that may be done by an over fastidious niceness of behaviour, I may cite a rather curious case I happen to know, where a mother, was so afraid of nakedness, and disliking the sight of her own body, that she actually put on a bathing dress when she had a bath even in the privacy of her own bath room. This mother had a son whose adult life was rendered miserable and his happiness to a great extent injured, by horrible and haunting obscene visions. Here, in very truth, the cleanness of the mother became the uncleanness of the son.

I must hasten on. I am bound to leave out much that might well be noticed, for the subject is very difficult and very wide. I hope, however, I have made clear to you the following truths:—

(1) That any education of children in sex that is to result in success in the after life cannot be fulfilled by the imparting of set and fixed lessons on sex-enlightenment, given either in the home or in the school. (2) That this education is concerned with the entire emotional life of the child. (3) That it is continuous and unceasing. (4) And that it is a work of such complexity that for even the wisest mistakes are certain and success uncertain.

Above all else, I am sure we have to avoid an easy and lazy optimism.

And with such perils awaiting the incautious, is it any wonder that the chief element of safety often is a negative one—non-interference? By non-interference the two chief factors leading to emotional disturbance and ill-health may almost certainly be avoided; thwarted wishes are not thrust back, and repressed to work harm in the psyche, causing mental and bodily ill-health which often does not manifest itself for many years; development is not hurried on too rapidly, so that necessary primitive stages of growth are omitted or hastened over too quickly, causing, not infrequently, in the later years of life, a regression backwards to primitive and uncivilised conduct.

When interference becomes necessary it must be given wisely and with due understanding of the child's position. I mean it must be the right instruction for the special child at that stage of its growth—not at all what the adult thinks it ought to be taught or would like to teach it. There can be no fixed rules as to sex teaching; no maxims laid down that can safely be always followed.

Take, for instance, the one apparently simple matter of satisfying the child's certain and right curiosity at the different stages of its growth, by telling it the facts of birth, and, as it grows older, explaining the difficulties that most certainly will arise in the mind of every boy and girl in regard to these questions. So far I have said little about this matter because most people say much; holding it as the one thing implied by sex education, whereas I regard it, as I have tried to make plain, as a limited, though certainly important duty in connection with that education, which should be fulfilled by parents, and within certain limitations, by teachers in the schools.

But here, again, I am bound to utter warnings. There must be no over-forcing of knowledge not sought for by the child, this is at least as injurious to the emotional growth as over-forcing is to the intellectual growth. Any one who has read Jung's account of his analysis of little Anna, will know what I mean. Little Anna became troubled and nervous, worried about the birth of a little brother or sister (I forget which). Telling her the truth did not help her, and it took Professor Jung many months of patient work with the child to get to the bottom of exactly what was troubling her. The most urgent rule for the mother in this matter is this: never to arouse sexual curiosity but to watch for its spontaneous expression and always satisfy it when it is present. This of course is the same as saying, always tell the child all the truth it wants to know. The difficulty here, of course, is that so rarely is the child able to ask for the knowledge he (or she) wants.

What above all else it is necessary is for the mother to watch for the child's unconscious betrayal of its own curiosity. I mean by this, that some unconsidered remark or act is the surest hope of finding just what part of the problem is troubling him (or her) at that time; in almost all cases there is a personal element of jealousy, unknown to the child or carefully hidden, which is directed against one or other parent, usually the father, or against some brother or sister. This is why the intellectual teaching of the facts of birth, though necessary, does not help very much and often disastrously fails.

As I am trying all the time to force upon you, the real sex education is an emotional education, that is why it is so difficult. I may make this plainer by means of an illustration which I give in my book on "Sex Education and National Health." It was told me by a very wise mother of her way of dealing with her son, who was, I think, about fourteen years old. This son showed he was thinking, and was evidently worried, about the very small families of one or at the most two children, or the childless marriages, common among his mother's friends. He did not, however, speak of his trouble directly; instead he beat round the question, somewhat in the manner of a shying horse. After this had gone on for some time, he one day asked his mother if her friends were more delicate (meaning, of course, more refined) than other people. His mother was aware of what was troubling him; she knew what he really wanted to know was whether married people lived in celibacy when they had not children. She wisely told him the plain facts and for him at that time curiosity was quieted.

A boy of nine had a dream which he told his parents. His mother was in a shop, and a man on a bicycle, dressed as an officer came along the road; he, the little boy, rushed to the bicycle, stopped it, flung the man off, and killed him. In telling the dream the boy said, "I prevented him getting to mother." This dream is so clear that I need not wait to interpret it beyond saying that the father of the boy was an officer. It will cause no surprise to anyone, with even a rudimentary knowledge of the emotional troubles of children, to know that this boy developed serious nervous symptoms.

It has seemed worth while to record these two instructive little stories, as a means of illustrating the kind of incident which furnishes the guide with regard to the nature of the trouble to be looked for, and shows in the first case as well the kind of help a watchful and instructed parent can give to relieve the trouble prevailing in the minds of the young. Dreams should always be noted, they throw the sharpest light on the child's emotional conflicts. I must again urge the necessity of the parent paying the closest attention to the child's prattle, to watching carefully his games and his behaviour, for in this way only can the clue be found to make it possible to give the kind of instruction or treatment that is wanted. I may give a few instances. Such things as the frequent childish desire to sit up with father and mother, the calling for the mother at night under the plea of fear are very certain signs of active jealousy. Again the very usual unwillingness of the child to grow up arises out of the inability to meet the necessity of separating the self from the protective tenderness of the mother. The child is always tending to turn back to safety, and, if this is encouraged by the mother, the child in after life will be unable to meet the necessities of adult action. The too fond mother perpetuates the childhood of her son or her daughter.

What the parents can do is to watch the child, and to learn themselves, in order to have the knowledge to clear up difficulties as these appear, and then it may be possible to remove obstructions to growth. Further, they can place within the child's reach the materials—the sand and clean messy things to play with—machines to pull to pieces, swords to fight with, dolls to play with—every child will need different materials, by which, to a certain extent, liberation can be found from their primitive instincts, by giving them a free and harmless expression. In fact the real work of the parent may be likened to that of the stage scene-shifter and property manager.

Parental power guides the early years of the child like a higher controlling fate. But when the boy or girl begins to grow up there begins also the conflict between the home attachments and the need to break away in order to free the growing soul from the spell of the family. It is the war between the generations. The frequent and often very deep depression of puberty arises from this struggle. And there are the many other, and often very disturbing, symptoms, which are rooted in the difficulty of the new adjustments. The boy or girl tries often to separate himself (or herself) as much as possible from his family; he (or she) may even estrange themselves from their parents but inwardly this only binds them more firmly to the family ties. The outward break must be regarded as a dangerous sign of the inner conflict which the unselfish wisdom of the parents ought to be able to aid.

I cannot follow this important matter further. But I would wish to say that this is the time for the teacher to step forward and take up the work begun by the parent. The parents at this period are often hindrances to the child, they must push their children away from them in order to help the growing souls to gain their liberation.

The uncertain and, as I fear they may seem, unsatisfactory conclusions that must result from any honest inquiry into this difficult question of helping the young at the start of their life's journey, is due in part to the fact that, even yet, and in spite of all the new knowledge that has been gained in the last few years, we know very little about the child's emotional processes. Unfortunately our knowledge is not sufficient to make it possible for any dogmatic statements to be placed even tentatively before parents. There can be no ready-made prescriptions, no certain cures. We do not even know where the greatest trouble lies, whether it is in the parents and the teachers—the adults who fail to understand the child; or in the child, who fights away from the understanding that those who love and train him are able to offer. We do know, however, that the difficulties on the part of the child are very great—much greater than most of us (whether we are parents or teachers)—satisfied in an easy grown-up optimism, have cared to realise. In many ways we—the adults—the parents and the teachers, we who are a generation behind the children and already have been through the long, struggling, upward journey, by which they are now travelling, ought to manage our love and our training for them more carefully, more sympathetically, and more intelligently. I say intelligently, because the sins committed in love against children are more lastingly harmful than many of the sins committed under neglect or even under unkindness.

Thus, the final word I have to say to parents in regard to their children is this:

Do not love your children too possessively.

Try to understand and respect them—realise their existence as individuals with interests and needs apart from yourself. If necessary send them from you. Do not love your children for your own satisfaction, but for their good, and to help them to establish, with as little disaster as possible, their own lives.

SEX INSTRUCTION

THE AGE AT WHICH KNOWLEDGE SHOULD BE GIVEN

A story is recorded of a father and mother in ancient Greece, who, being concerned for the welfare of their only son, went to a renowned teacher and asked him to educate and take full charge of their child. "How old is your son?" questioned the teacher.

"Just three!"

The sage shook his head. "I am sorry but you have come to me too late: the boy's character is decided already."

I was reminded of this most instructive story as I read the account of the evidence given by the Rev. the Hon. Ed. Lyttelton, before the Birth Rate Commission of the National Council of Public Morals. For while I agree wholeheartedly with the late headmaster of Eton College as to the necessity of instructing the young in the facts of sex, I disagree, with his view as to the method of the teaching and, even more I disagree emphatically, as to the age at which instruction should begin.

Dr. Lyttelton holds that the first lessons should be given at the age of nine years, when the boy ought to be taught the facts of maternity, this knowledge to be supplemented by further teaching at the age of twelve or thirteen explaining the even more important (for the boy) facts of paternity.

Now it is here that I venture to disagree, and think that Dr. Lyttelton has fallen into the very common error of underestimating the child's intelligence and boundless curiosity. It is in the very early nursery days that sex education is most urgently needed. To wait until the age of nine years has been reached is often to wait too late. In a vast number of cases, it is locking the stable door after the horse has been stolen.

In all children the activity of the intelligence begins to work at a very early age, and parents, who are not willfully blind, must know that this activity tends to manifest itself in an inquisitive desire to know many elementary facts of life, which are dependent upon sex. The primary and most universal of these desires is the desire to know where "the new baby comes from." A child of four or even younger, may begin to ask questions on this matter quite simply and spontaneously. The degree of curiosity, as also the frankness with which it is expressed, will differ, of course, in different children, but I am certain this curiosity is present and at times active in all children. If they do not question their elders, they will certainly puzzle over the matter themselves; often they will talk with older companions, and gain the information they are seeking in the worst possible way.

Thus the first teacher of the child must be the mother, the one who is most constantly with the child, tending him in washing, undressing, and in all the daily needs of his little body. It is the mother who ought to be the child's supreme trainer.

Few of us understand the confusion and hurt that may be caused by a mother's stupid silence and even more stupid hints and evasions and made-up fables. The false stories of babies brought by the doctor or the stork, or a little sister or brother found under the gooseberry bush are never believed. While the fantastic ideas of birth, that the child makes up for himself, fix their untruth into the immature minds. And afterwards they cannot be checked, owing to childish concealments, which always spring up so rapidly to meet any expression of adult reticence. These birth-fantasies, though the child seems to out-grow them, are not really forgotten but remain active in the unconscious mind. In this way, trouble is often started that will be determinative of the gravest evils in the later adult life.

Parents are greatly to blame for not answering the questions of their children, and being blind to their natural curiosity. And I would emphasise again that this curiosity is present even when no questions are asked. There need be no spoken words to make the child feel that its questions are discouraged. All adults are surprisingly ignorant of the affectability of children—their quick response to every kind of influence.

In the case of the birth of another child—an usurper who takes the older child's place—this affectability is exceedingly acute on account of the emotional disturbance, in excitement and possible jealousy. And by means of the adult attitude, the very certain interest and investigation of the child into what is happening may so easily become confused and connected with what is shameful and wrong; and the trouble is aided, and usually in the worst possible manner, by the sharpest observations and deductions made by the child *from unconsidered actions and overheard remarks* of parents, and of servants and other adults—none of whom have any idea of the child's watchfulness or his curiosity in this matter.

We think little children are not interested in birth because we do not want them to be interested. And they, with the almost uncanny sagacity which children show, understand this desire only too well and too quickly.

I had a striking illustration of this curious adult blindness quite recently. Two mothers, who were sisters, were pregnant at the same time. Each mother told me privately that *her children* were not interested in the event or in any way curious, but that *her sister's children* were curious and wanting to find out what was happening. It would have been useless to tell these mothers the truth. Yet both of them were intelligent. They believed that their own children had no curiosity because *they wished to believe this, not because it was true.*

Thwarted curiosity is one of the most frequent causes of emotional disturbance in the first years of life. Do we not all know children who as they get older exhibit an unreasoning curiosity about everything, opening drawers, looking into the envelopes of other people's letters, searching excitedly for what they do not want. We want to ask the question: Why does the child do this? What is it that urges him to act like a "Peeping Tom?" For he is urged. You will find this habit of needless prying almost impossible to check. It may persist into adult life. Do not we all know grown-ups who cannot refrain from prying, always curious, they are, on all occasions, seeking for knowledge they do not want.

This seeking action is symbolic. It implies that the search for the thing that is not wanted, the curiosity over something of no interest at all, is a substitute action for something that at one time was wanted—something about which knowledge *was desired,* and desired so much that it *would not be denied*. It was a curiosity so real that the thwarting of it has started emotional trouble of which these searching acts and persisting curiosity are the symbol or sign.

This substitute formation is one of the commonest emotional processes in children. The child pries, open drawers and letters, collects useless objects, aimlessly searches for knowledge he does not want *because there is some knowledge he wants tremendously badly, but cannot speak about*. That is why he persists in his habits of peeping and prying in spite of your scoldings and punishments. He must persist, unless you deaden his character so terribly by your ill-judged repression that even this substitute relief is closed. Your child will then, probably, find some other make-believe comfort; he will bite his nails, pick his nose, or other much worse habits may begin, or again the emotional disturbance may be so acute that it becomes impossible for the child to face, so that he fails in achieving any kind of symbolic replacement. The thwarted and emotionally over-charged curiosity is thrust back into the psyche where it remains a cause of ill-health of body and uncleanness of mind, until that time in the adult years, when the harvest of tares is reaped from the bad seed that has been sown.

The parents have the greatest responsibility, as I have said already. A child of four or even younger may begin to ask questions of its mother, simply and spontaneously. *It is the child who must guide the parent.* But again I would give warning. The mother must not be over-eager, or she will fall easily into the error of stimulating instead of quieting the child's restless inquiring mind. The child at the age when such questions will first be asked and should be answered, will very quickly tire of any information that may be given to it. It will break off to run away and play and will interrupt the most beautiful and carefully prepared lessons. And if the mother is wise she will never go beyond the interest of the child, or the satisfying *and nothing further*, of the special curiosity which at that special time is occupying the child. If this course is pursued the child will probably continue to ask for information—though there can be no certainty that this desirable result will follow. But where such opportunities arise the right kind of sex instruction can be attempted. For the mother will be able to give answers in natural conversation, which will not force information not sought for by the child. When so treated, it will be found that children are not over-burdened by the subject, they will interrupt and break away from the answer to the question they have asked to speak about toy soldiers or dolls. This, to me, is the immense value of this form of teaching: the child has the information, and yet does not trouble about it when it is not to the point. Such a result can never be gained by means of set talks or fixed lessons, especially if these are mixed up with warnings, and much vague talk of things that the child neither cares for or understands.

I should, however, be giving a wrong impression if I left the matter here, so that this answering of children's questions seemed to be a simple matter. It is not simple. For each child, as for each adult the problems of sex are personal problems. And the child whose problem is the hardest—who most urgently needs help, will hardly ever ask questions. Instruction in sex is not *and never can be* like teaching the child about other things. That is what so many of the modern advocates of sex education so entirely forget.

In every child, as I have tried to show you there are hidden conflicts of jealousy, of love, of hate, which determine beforehand its response to the teaching that is given by the parents.

I cannot here treat at all adequately this difficult question; it is one on which I have written elsewhere (*Mother and Son, Sex Education and National Health, The Mind of the Naughty Child*) I can say only what I have emphasised already that from the start to the end, *sex education is an emotional education.* That, of course, is why it is so difficult.

There is, in my opinion, too firm a belief in the efficacy of formal instruction. The way is not so easy as this to discharge our debt to the young. And sometimes I fear that parental talks about sex, in particular when such talks are delayed until the boy or the girl is reaching puberty, or until the time when the dangers of school life have to be met, involving, as it must, a sudden breaking through of the silence of years, may work for harm instead of for good. That this is so in the case of some boys and girls I know to be true. You see you cannot grow flowers in a soil choked already with weeds.

THE MYTH OF THE VIRTUOUS SEX

A day or two ago I was passing one of the great London schools at the afternoon hour when the boys were released. I write "boys," but among them were many of sixteen, seventeen, or even eighteen years who looked almost men.

On the street side, two flappers, quite young—not more, I should judge, than fifteen, stood with their faces pressed between the iron rails and watched the exit of the boys. Certainly they were not nice girls; they invited with smiles, they giggled, they ogled, they gestured. There could, I think, be no mistake as to the purpose of the girls.

I am glad to record that no single boy took the slightest notice of them.

Now this very unpleasant incident has set me thinking. I am oppressed with feelings of responsibility; yes—and also of shame. If I am to be honest I must accept here, as in all relations between the two sexes, the validity of the mans' plea that rings—yes, and will continue to ring—through the centuries: "The woman tempted me!"

Now, though we may accept this responsibility in theory, most often we repudiate it in practice. From time to time—and the intervals are not long apart—efforts are made to pass new laws which are supported by many virtuous people—laws, whose one purpose is to increase the punishments of men for offences against young girls.

I am in whole-hearted sympathy with any changes in our law that will afford greater protection to young girls. I cannot, however, refuse to see the reverse side of the question. It is proposed to raise the age of consent for girls, while at the same time a woman is not to be held responsible for seducing a boy who is much younger than herself. This is unjust.

Why should we afford a period of protection longer for the girl than for the boy?

It may, of course, be argued that the boy is better able to look after himself. This is not true.

The girl grows up more quickly always than the boy; emotionally she is far more developed, and, therefore, should be more, and not less, responsible than he is. I have no doubt about this at all.

No boy knows very much about love until some girl or woman has taught him.

Of course, the view of the evil nature of men, and of women as always the victim, is one that can hardly fail to be pleasing to women, depending, as it does, on their moral superiority, which stamps them as Amazons of

Purity, on the glorious mountain heights of virtue, from where they must send down climbing ropes and ladders, in the form of prohibitions and regulations and new laws, to pull men up out of the deep valleys of vice.

But if we inquire more honestly into this question of men's sins, we shall find that it is not they who are wholly responsible. There is little difference between men's virtue and women's virtue.

Almost unceasingly in our streets women are tempting men.

Always there is the invitation near: "Come and make love to me." To be provocative is the one simple rule of many women's lives. Men's admiration is a necessity to their very existence.

True, in the after results, the woman may be, and, indeed, often is, the victim—has to pay the heavier price; but at the start she is the leader of the assault.

The essential fact in every relationship of the sexes is the woman's power over the man, and it is the misuse of this power that is the beginning of sin.

Do not think I am unfair. Most men, I know, are not only tolerant of women's wiles; they like them. But most men succumb, I believe, against their will, and often against their inclination, to the tyranny of their own aroused passions.

Men's chivalry, as well as their pride, has woven a cloak of silence on this question of the temptation they are so frequently called upon to resist and this silence has protected women—even the worst.

Let us alter our laws to help girls by all means. Yet, let us be just. There is such a thing as too much temptation for a boy—temptation that a woman has no right to give.

SENTIMENTAL TAMPERING WITH DIFFICULT PROBLEMS:

WITH SOME REMARKS ON SEX FAVOURITISM

It is sometimes difficult to have patience with the proposals that are brought forward, so frequently and with such persistent zeal, to amend our Criminal Law. One cannot doubt the sincerity of these efforts to improve our disordered moral conditions. But something more than good-will is required. There is such a thing as over-haste in righteousness.

Besides, the attitude taken by these scavengers of conduct is almost always sentimental and one-sided. It is also dishonest. I say so, because almost without exception, they fail entirely to meet the true facts of the evils they attempt to cure. As reformers they seem to have but one idea; if they have more, they keep them secret, for they agitate but for one object.

Morality is a word that has been wrested from its true meaning of the whole duty of man in his social character and limited to the one narrow application of sexual conduct. It is curious and significant. It is as if we transferred to others some judgment which unconsciously was imposed from within.

Yet obviously the strongest impediment against effective reform lies just here—in this blindness to reality; this separation from the truth. I need not wait to enlarge upon this further, it is impossible to contradict. To judge blindly is to judge upon a lie.

Would you ask me to give you examples?

There is, to take one illuminative instance, the long continued and still unsettled agitation for raising the age of consent for girls. Those who are chiefly eager for this reform invariably evince frenzied zeal, combined with the most curious and deplorable ignorance of the real facts. I cannot for a moment believe that they are in the least degree, consciously blind. But that does not alter the fact that they are blind. Instead of facing the situation squarely with knowledge and due consideration of all the complicated conditions, they ignore every thing they do not want to see. They wallow in sex-righteousness.

Consider again the controversy that raged now sometime back, with regard to the White Slave Traffic. The sudden frenzy. The unproved stories of the trapping of girls! The clamour for legislative measures! Every moral reformer became obsessed.

The instinctive attitude of the one-ideaed reformer had a unique chance of displaying itself, and one marvelled at the almost curious enthusiasm, mated to inexperience, with which the subject was approached. While the most offensive feature of the agitation was the sex-obsession, which gave rise to the silly notion of the helpless perfection of women and the dangerous opposite view of the indescribable imperfections of men. It is no exaggeration to say that every sense of reality was lost in white clouds of virtue.

I would wish to make it plain that I am not judging these questions either on one side or the other. What I desire to show is the danger of a prejudiced view. And the danger is particularly active in connection with all these attempts at changing the law, in order to give greater protection to women and girls, while, at the same time, boys are left unprotected.

This unpopular view of the need to protect the boy from the girl—the man from woman—the temptress of man—is not usually brought forward. Yet, it is a view of the situation, seen from a different side, that cannot be neglected. The evidence is overwhelming of girls of sixteen years and even younger tempting boys of the same age as well as those older than themselves. If in such cases the boy is to be punished and the girl treated as a wronged and helpless victim, not only will a great unjustice be done, but there will be a very certain danger of graver demoralisations.

This truth of the woman's power, which depends upon Nature and not upon law, the supporters of a one-sided alteration of our criminal law too often fail to face.

I am reminded here of a little incident that happened many years ago. I had quarrelled seriously with a man, who before I had always liked and respected, for what I then considered was his light treatment of a certain girl who was my friend. She had written and told me her side of this occurrence.

Very well I recall what he said: "You don't understand. She asked for it." Then, when I pressed him further, he went on. "A man always treats a girl in the way she wants him to do."

Now, one of the greatest troubles in connection with all sex-legislation to-day arises from this fact that *women do not understand*. They are inexperienced and in too great a hurry. They think they can cure old evils with quick penny-in-the slot reforms. There is still a chivalry that protects women and shields their ignorance. These illusions are maintained, even by men of the world, who are acquainted with all the complex difficulties. It is the romantic view, a kind of male blindness that nothing seems to cure. Women must be protected from men, who are the great offenders in all sexual sins. Often I have marvelled at the acceptance by men of a view of the sex-conflict so highly untrue, though flattering to women, depending as it does on their entirely unproved moral superiority.

And here I wish to ask your attention to a consideration of the question that is very rarely appreciated. I regard it as exceedingly important. Those who are possessed with a frenzy for protecting girls ought to remember that there is still greater necessity to protect boys. It is forgotten that the young girl is not usually in constant close relations with other men than her father and brothers. She has to be guarded only from the *outside lover*, whom *in the first beginning of intimacy she could, if she wished, easily repel.*

The reverse is the case with boys. In a sense, they cannot escape from situations of danger. At school, in lodgings, even at home, in sickness and also in health; on every occasion opportunities are provided that make abuse exceedingly easy. The part played in the sexual initiation of boys by servants, by lodging and boarding-house keepers, and by other women who have to tend, and feed and mend for them is much larger than is credited. It is folly to close our eyes to the evils that so often arise. *Probably every man who is a seducer of women was himself first seduced by a woman.*

In spite of the emancipation upon which women pride themselves, in spite of much theoretical knowledge, yes, in spite of social and rescue work—where, it should be noted, they hear the woman's story but only in the rarest cases the man's story—almost all women lead a shielded life. Much that happens is outside their experience—as long as they are virtuous. This sets definite limits to their knowledge and their power of comprehension. And this again explains the continued belief in the woman's notion that, *in all cases,* the girl is the victim of the man.

It would be nearer the truth to reverse the position. Girls need to be taught their great and unavoidable responsibility. They should be trained to be protectors rather than to seek protection. *Men will treat them as they want to be treated.*

Let us now, for a moment, be practical and consider if there is any reason we can discover, which will explain why we hear so much more about the seduction of girls and the sins of men than we ever do about the other side—the tempting by women and girls, and the seduction of boys. The answer is simple. The boy will not talk about what happens to him if he is led into a sexual offence at an early age. This is true also to a large extent of the man. But the boy especially considers he ought to have known: also he is much more self-conscious. Then he expects to be blamed for not resisting, whatever the circumstances. He will probably not tell anyone, unless the girl does so, until years afterwards.

I know a schoolboy who was seduced by a woman relation years older than himself, in a very shameful way. This boy was of high character and very sensitive; he suffered in ways impossible to relate here, but he never told anyone until about ten years afterwards, when he told the woman he was to marry.

Now, if this case had been reversed and a young schoolgirl had been the victim of a male relative, I am fairly confident the fact would not have been concealed. Girls, even if not wholly innocent, almost always will tell, because it has at all times been allowed to them to blame the man. They thus can count on sympathy. This means much more than usually is reckoned with.

Let me give a less tragic instance of a different and humourous character. A schoolboy, about seventeen years old, was waiting for a motor-bus in which he was going home. He was a dreamy boy and a bus came up and, lost in his thoughts, he did not take it. He was brought back to reality by a girl accosting him. "I waited, too," she said. "You, are glad arn't you? You would like me to go in the bus with you."

She smiled up at him: but he was not to be caught.

"I don't care, the hell, what you do as long as you don't expect me to pay your fare!"

That silenced her and sent her away. But how easily, had the boy been a less confident type, the incident might have taken a different course. And then, if disaster had followed, the boy would be blamed, the girl would be pitied. There is an enormous amount of sex unfairness.

I could recount many further cases in proof of how almost always it is the girl (or the woman) who takes the first steps in forming these friendships. Men, at least, will know that I speak the truth. And yet this fiction of the greater virtue of the woman is persistently maintained: while the man is condemned as being nearer the devil and the beast.

I know that the many horrible cases of criminal assault upon children will be quoted against me, in proof of the justice of this heavy condemnation of men. Please do not think that I am in any way unaware of the awfulness of these crimes. The protection of little children is the one matter on which I feel most deeply. But there can be no fair comparison between this class of crime and the ordinary cases of seduction, whether we believe it is the man who seduces the woman, or the other way round, the woman who tempts and excites the boy or the man. In the one case an unhappy and terrible degenerate is passion-driven into the commission of an atrocity, in the other there is, and, indeed, must be to some extent, a mutual purpose, usually with some calculation and a certain deliberate choice.

That is why it is so false to reality to regard the one partner as a helpless victim. It is really a position that is impossible and ridiculous. Are we to believe that all women are impotent and imbecile weaklings incapable of resisting men? The truth is that in slandering men we only slander women with the backward swing of the same blow.

THE SEDUCTION OF MEN

Quite recently an action has been brought in the High Courts by a wife against a woman for the seduction of her husband. It is the first time a charge of this kind has been heard in an English court of law, though, I believe, such actions are not unknown in the newer lands of America and Canada.

The case is one of very special interest, and opens up many questions that go right down to the deepest problems of the relationships of men and women.

As we should expect, the action failed. It was held that the man had not been seduced. He was not enticed away from his wife by "the other woman," rather, it was the other way round. The man, not the woman, must be held responsible; she had yielded to him only at his desire, after persuasion and against her will.

But is this true?

As already in the two previous essays I have emphasised, perhaps over-emphasised, the accepted, very sentimental and peculiar judgment in all these cases. The woman the victim: the man the seducer. He the active sinner: she the passive sufferer. All the blame to be heaped on to him: all the pity to be given to her.

Really it is difficult, as so frequently I have stated, to have patience at this shelving of the real facts. It seems to be forgotten entirely how tremendous is the power of the woman in all love relationships. Why a man under the influence of a woman he loves is as easily led and as devoid of all will-power as a young child. Indeed, he becomes the child of the woman, as soon as, and for as long as, he loves her. He is her's to make or to destroy. She strengthens him enormously or irreparably injures and weakens his resistance. She can hold him to the hardest duty and keep him in the fine path of right doing. It is she leads him, not he who leads her, into the easier ways of love.

Yes, it is women who shape the souls of men as it is women who gave them birth.

That is why this view of the man's responsibility in love being greater than the woman's is so singularly untrue. If we inquire at all truthfully into this question of seduction, it is obvious that not the man but the woman is the more responsible. For one thing, she knows so much more about love, from the beginning, and *without being taught*, than a man ever knows. Most often it is the woman who takes the first step, breaks down the first barrier. Always there is the invitation which unceasingly she gives, whether consciously or unconsciously expressed—"Come and love me."

Her dress, her movements—all invite love. To be provocative is however, little she knows it, the one fixed simple rule of her life. In the end, and indeed, sometimes very soon the position may be reversed, but at the start assuredly the woman holds the cards and can make the first move in the love-game. She is the pursuer, far more often and far more truly, than the pursued. Too often she directs a continuous attack.

Her relation to the man is comparable to that of a magnet to a heap of iron filings.

Love to a woman so often, when she is young, is less an affair of passion than of excitement. It gratifies her insatiable desire for power. The boy or the man more certainly is driven by love. This is his principal motive. While the girl often starts on the adventure for the sake of experiment and because she wants amusement. She pursues love almost as a game. Passion plays a part only in the second degree. Not infrequently, in the midst of love, the coldness of her heart is plainly apparent.

This may seem a hard saying. I believe it is true.

Seduction as the crime of the man alone cannot, I am convinced, be accepted, in any case without great caution. It is, as I have said several times already, so comfortable to place the sins of sex on men. But I doubt very much if any woman *can be seduced against her will.*

I must insist again that excitement and escape from dullness, as also the joy in receiving presents and having "a good time," are the principal motives that first lead girls into illegal relations.

Sometimes it is worse than this.

Many women, seducers of men—women who draw men from their wives and their homes, and their duty, are nothing but cold experimentors. They are speculators in love. They do this for delight of power, in the same way as men are speculators in business.

Perhaps the position is unavoidable.

The subjection of man is a necessity to some women's existence. Love is to them a similar feeling to love of the chase. They cannot keep from pursuing men. It is, as I have said, an expression of the ever increasing demand for excitement. Conquest in love gives to women the opportunities for the fulfilment of themselves, which men gain in many different departments of life.

But no man, I think, could satisfy completely the craving for dominion, which the delusive humility of his desire awakens in this type of woman. Then when she commits the error, from a womanly point of view, of hunting down her man; leading him on by helping him too much—seducing him, instead of waiting for him and drawing him slowly and unconsciously by her love, she awakens the same instinct for dominion and thirst for excitement in the man. It is then that the man becomes a seducer of other women. It is the lust to devour, to crush, quickened into being by suggestion. It explains, I believe, the cruelty of all wild love.

PLAYING WITH LOVE

Many girls to-day try deliberately to keep love light. Shrewd enough to understand the heavy claims of serious love affairs that lead to marriage, they prefer flirtations of weeks only—episodes that are a secret and, as it were, detachable part of their lives.

It is a dangerous state.

Emotional power and the enjoyment of the simple pleasures of life are dried up by such constant stimulation. A new diet of excitement must always be provided. The object of life is to cheat time and to crowd out boredom. Whatever is going on they must be in it from a jazz dance or river picnic to a church bazaar.

In the old days it used to be only duties for girls—now it is rights and pleasure with the demand to be left to make their own lives. There is a turning away from duty; a hatred of anything dull.

Girls as I have just shown you want love as an experience and to provide the always desired excitement. They do not want to marry and to settle down.

Thus while condescending to fascinate men, while deliberately seeking attention these young women still hold themselves in hand. Intending to exploit life to the uttermost they find love amusing, but they fight always against its being a vocation.

There is calculation and dangerous hardiness in their attitude to their lovers.

Their transitory love affairs are, indeed, regarded in very much the same way as formerly they were regarded by the average young men—as enjoyable and thrilling incidents of which they are ashamed only when they are talked about and blamed.

With no sex conscience, these wantons of excitement have no consciousness of womanly responsibility. Each new affair affords an eagerly snatched tribute to a colossal and restless vanity.

This is one type of woman who to-day plays with love.

There are as well other girls of a different character, less concerned with pleasure, less consciously vain, more emotional, and to men more interesting. They are incessantly thinking of their own personalities; and, for this reason, they are equally, even if not more, harmfully destructive in the utter misery they often create.

These are the girls who are always emotion hunting.

Impossible to tell what are their pseudo-feelings. A sort of sterile passion, which expends itself in their failure to know, and find, what they want.

They do not wish consciously to escape the responsibilities of marriage; indeed they seek unceasingly the perfect man to whom they may surrender their freedom. But they suffer from a formless discontent that rots into every love and prevents them finding satisfaction.

Consumed with haggard restlessness, such girls pass their days in a dangerous state of expectancy and nervous tiredness. Eternally they are unsatisfied without knowing why.

Born spiritual adventurers, these worshippers of emotionalism, attitudinising and thinking perpetually of themselves, desire at all cost a position in the limelight. They love romantically, but rarely are they strong enough to obey their inclinations. Such girls are out on an eternal quest; and, every now and again, they believe they have found the ideal man they are seeking. Then they discover they have not found him, so their search is taken up anew. While often their insistent egoism, which causes them to ignore the rights of others and all social obligations, drives them into dangerous corners; does not give them a chance; turns them to use mean weapons of deceit; forces them into false situations that too often close around them like a trap.

Many other nobler types, besides these two, have been playing with love.

Girls of profound and steadfast emotional nature are rare. The great majority of girls certainly are not entirely light-minded, but they are less serious, more noisily determined to do what they want, to get what they can both out of men and out of life. They are very like children, playing at desperate rebels, who take up weapons to use far more deadly than they know.

All this playing with love is detestable—all of it. It bears witness to a poverty of emotion and a shameful shirking of responsibility.

Women are the custodians of manners in love. The future rests with them. And this responsibility cannot safely be set aside, dependent as it is on forces active long before human relations were established—forces which press on women back and back through the ages.

Yes, woman has laid upon her the sacred necessity of seriousness in all that is connected with Love. It is a duty imposed upon her by Nature, and one that she cannot escape. That is why there is so much danger in these restless neurotic years, when girls are too excited to be serious.

SECTION III
MARRIAGE AND OTHER RELATIONSHIPS

IS PASSIONATE LOVE THE SUREST FOUNDATION FOR MARRIAGE?

"There is no subject," says Bernard Shaw in the preface to *Getting Married*, "on which more dangerous nonsense is talked and thought than marriage." And though I disagree rather violently with Mr. Shaw's views about marriage, he is right here. We do talk dangerous nonsense, which need not matter very much, if we did not think absurdly, and so inevitably have to pay the fruit in wrong action. This explains, I think, our curious levity, our unhappiness, and fierce refusal to face facts.

We have infested our ideals with the poison of pleasure and turned away from essential things. Marriage is not a religion to us—it is a sport.

I say this quite deliberately. I am sure we know better how to engage a servant, how to buy a house, how to set up in business—how, indeed, to do every unimportant thing in life, than we know how to choose a partner in marriage. We require a character with our cook or our butler, we engage an expert to test the drains of our house, we study and work to prepare ourselves for business, but in marriage we take no such sensible precautions; we even pride ourselves that we do not take them. We speak of *falling in love*, and we *do fall*.

The conventions of to-day are false; they are bound up with concealments or with an equally untruthful openness. It does not, however, follow from this that mere destruction will be enough, that everyone's unguided ignorance will lead to success and freedom. The *laisser faire* system is as false in the realm of marriage as it is in industry and economics. While equally false, though this is rarely recognised, is the modern spiritual view of marriage that love can be found only in perfect harmony of character between the wife and the husband, *and is independent of duty*. It is true that love differs from lust in its deeper insight into the personality, deeper interest in character, as opposed to the inexpressive smooth outline and "untrained" physical beauty of the body. But the character and intellect may be studied and loved as self-centeredly, as much with a view to the enjoyment of mental excitement, as the body itself.

Of all of which what is the moral? This:

In marriage, as in other things, we fasten our chains about our own necks. We do not find what we desire because we do not know what we want.

The very word love is used in so general and indiscriminate a way to denote sometimes the most transitory impulse and sometimes the most intense feeling, that a mass of misunderstanding arises. The emotion which most often passes under the name of love is a maudlin, sickly sentiment or passion founded on hypocrisy, which means nothing at bottom but the desired enjoyment of a passion which is felt but not understood, and which professes to be everything but that which it is in reality.

With more courage to face truth, we should have a surer ideal; there would be much less sentimentality, but much deeper feeling about marriage. Our romance is slightly vulgar. Vulgarity is a sign of weakness of spirit, that spirit which is "the life that carves out life" as Nietzsche says.

We associate romance with courtship and not with marriage. "Thank God our love-time is ended!" cried a north country bride on the day that marriage ended her long engagement.

Now, I do not know whether this delightful story is true, but it does illustrate the attitude of many ordinary couples, whose love adventure ends at the very hour it should begin.

Every marriage ought to be a succession of courtships.

A very slight knowledge of existing marriages is sufficient to convince even the most optimistic believer that true mating is hard. I do not believe that most marriages are unhappy, but I do know that only the very few are happy. With many perhaps, and even with those who are passionate lovers, the attraction of sex always seems to fall short of its end; it draws the two together in a momentary self-forgetfulness, but for the rest it seems rather to widen their separateness. They are secret to one another in everything; united only in the sexual embrace.

Can we, then, ever find perfect love? Is it not like exercise of the body? You can develop it to a certain point, but not beyond, without danger; and very slowly, with continued patient effort. Do we not need exercise of the soul? I do not know. Often I feel I know nothing. To some men and women it is all simple enough, a woman is just a woman and a man is a man. The trouble begins when any woman becomes the one desired woman and any man the one desired man.

There is gain and development in this selective tendency of Love—and yet, if I am right, there is terrible danger lurking in the application of this egoistic spiritual view.

We may not safely ask too much or too little from marriage or take too high or too low a view of it.

I am not very hopeful of improvement. At least, not for a long time, and never unless we learn to be more honest about ourselves and about love.

In fear, we have tried to keep the blinds down so that love may be decently obscured. Yet how can we ever begin to understand and deal with these problems of sex unless we will admit all the instincts and tendencies which ever lead us backwards to the more elemental phases of life? The deepest of the emotions is sex, and its actions, like all the emotions that are fundamental, may be traced into a thousand bye-paths of the ordinary experience of each one of us; it exercises its influence on every period of our development, and works subconsciously to control our actions in endless ways that we refuse to acknowledge.

Hence the conflicts which manifest themselves so strangely and so fiercely in our lives. The emotional-self refuses, at times, to be controlled by the reason-self. Restraint cannot do much, and indeed, often brings deeper evils. For our unconscious selves are stronger than all the pretenses and guards we have set up by our conscious wills, either as individuals to encourage our own conceit and egoism, or collectively as a so-called civilized people in the hope of controlling conduct.

That is why so much that is said to-day about sexual conduct is so foolish. The real question is not what *people ought to do*, but what they *actually do* and *want to do*, and, therefore, are likely *to go on doing*. It is these facts that the reformers of marriage almost always fail to face.

To me, one thing, at least, is certain, the romantic view of marriage has failed us.

But we cannot change the ideal of to-day unless we have ready a new ideal to inspire our conduct. We cannot destroy a sanctuary unless we first build a sanctuary.

There is a strange idea among some young people to-day that sexual happiness can be gained by breaking away from all the traditional bonds, it is the visible sign of our confusion as a people, and the want of happiness in our lives. The new generation should not set at naught the experience of the ages.

The individual household where both parents share in the common interest of bringing up the children, is the foundation on which marriage has been built up, and on which it must stand. If the conditions of the home are seriously changed, and the bearing and caring for children is no longer considered an essential part of marriage, a change in marriage itself will follow. I do not think you can hold the one if you let the other go. For Westermark is right, and children should not be regarded as the result of marriage, but marriage as the result of children. And love between men and women implies duties and responsibilities that go out beyond themselves; without this, even love of the most passionate kind, loses its quality and tends to become an ephemeral or even a corrupt thing.

There is much stupidity in the view of many reformers of marriage who fail to see that, however hard it is to live faithfully to the obligation, and unchecked responsibilities of love, the old ideal of marriage does so appeal to our emotional nature, that men and women are seriously unhappy in trying to destroy it.

Not all who cry "It is useless," can do without the limiting safeguards of children and of legal marriage. We still feel the serpent's sting of jealousy and the old questions, "Where do you come from?" "What have you been doing to-night?" "Who handled your body till daytime, while I watched and wept?" "In what bed did you lie and whom did you gladden with your smile?" are still felt, even if not uttered by the lips, of the most emancipated husbands and wives. For our sex-judgments are not intellectual, nor are they merely moral; they are not just questions of understanding and forgiving, but they are also physical, of the nerves, of the blood, of the fiercest instinct.

Fortunately it is easier to talk of love's freedom, than it is to act as if it ever could be free. And in spite of what advanced people say, some feeling of duty in sex will always exist as long as it hurts us at all to hurt others. The immorality that says, "Do what you desire irrespective of others," is as yet beyond most of us.

Attempts to solve these problems quickly are bound to fail. Intellectual revolutionists are, I think too hopeful with regard to what may be done to produce a harmony of sexual needs. The optimism that once prevailed in regard to economics is being transformed to sexual matters. Once people supposed that if every one followed his own interests a harmony would automatically establish itself in the economy of society. Now they tend to say the same about sex.

Intellectual views of life and what is right and wrong always act to break people into groups, each struggling to explain everything according to one theory, built on a single principle. And as the result of caring so much for one thing, people seem quite unable to grasp any facts that do not refer to their own particular reform; they are not able even to consider it as part of a world in which there is anything else. All the evil in marriage? is due to too large families and populations pressing upon the food supply, we are told by one class of enthusiasts, while others point to men's tyranny over women. Emancipation for women, with an equal moral standard, would have a magical effect: men are all bad say some. The father is a parasite, unnecessary except for his share in begetting the child; the mother is the one parent. All would be well if legal marriage were abolished and motherhood made free, is the view common among one class of reformers. Eugenical breeding and sterilisation of the unfit is the remedy brought forward by others. Many suggest economic changes and the endowment of motherhood.

But the matter is not so simple as these reformers seem to believe. And I doubt if any outward change is really capable of producing the prompt kind of penny-in-the-slot results that its supporters claim that it can. The complexity of marriage (in particular, the occurrence of sexual disharmonies so present and active for misery to-day) is ignored by all intellectual reformers. It is because they have no emotional hold on life as a whole that they find it easy to squeeze all life into their magic theories. For myself I can see no sure remedy—though in a later essay I shall try to suggest a palliative: but were I asked to state my deepest belief, I could say only "A few thousand years more of development, a growth towards consciousness and a fuller understanding of the meaning of life."

MARRIAGE REFORM

Many people seem to be in fear that any change in the marriage laws will destroy marriage. "Hands off! No tinkering with marriage!" they cry in a panic of timidity and moral anger.

I marvel at this want of faith. Do they, indeed, believe that the institution of marriage rests on a trembling quicksand, so that its supporters are compelled to build a scaffolding of lies to sustain its foundations?

The laws of marriage are only the register of what marriage is: they do not control marriage. There are no laws, for instance, to regulate the perfect love-unions of birds, whose faithfulness and family life present a beautiful and high standard of conduct.

Let there be no mistake here. I have been told that I wish to destroy permanent marriage, that I do not consider the welfare of children and the best interests of the race. I deny these charges; they are untrue.

My ideal of marriage is one that many will call old-fashioned. It demands the consecration of the mother in service to her husband, to their children, and the home. That is why I advocate the recognition and regulation of other forms of union, not because I have a low ideal, but to prevent the degradation of marriage by forcing into it those who do not desire, and, therefore, are unsuited for, its binding duties.

The immense failure of marriage to-day arises from the confusion of our desires and our ceaseless search for individual happiness. We have no firm ideal, no fixed standard of conduct either for women or for men. And the existence of many standards of what ought to be done; the liberty permitted to the man, the liberty permitted to the woman; if the wife shall continue her work or profession or remain at home dependent on the husband's earnings; whether the marriage shall be fruitful or sterile—these are but a few of the questions left undecided. And thus to leave men and women unguided, with their own ideas of what is good to do and what is evil, is the dry-rot very surely destroying the ideal of marriage.

Every couple starts anew and alone, and the way is too difficult for solitary experiments.

This modern delusion of looking at marriage as an individual affair is of course, the essence of the selfish, egocentric habit of life—it focuses desire on personal adventure and personal needs. With more courage to face the realities of love we should have a surer ideal. There would be less sentimentality, but much deeper feeling about marriage.

This, then, is what I would teach: No longer must marriage be regarded solely as a personal relationship. Marriage is a religious duty.

"To be mothers were women created, and to be fathers, men."

This was the ideal which gave the breath of life to marriage among the men and women in our earlier England, who were more fixed in character and less selfish than we are to-day.

It is this ideal we have lost.

TO-DAY'S IDEAS ON MARRIAGE

ARE WE SEEKING VAINLY AFTER HAPPINESS?

It will not do to dismiss this question with the old unreasoning condemnation of men; nor will it serve to talk of their polygamous nature and uncontrolled passions. Let us look at the matter a little more closely, and with greater regard to truth.

In marriage the woman dominates more often than usually is known. For one thing she has the children on her side. I think marriage is more of a duel than usually is acknowledged. One partner wins, kills the other, kills all that makes joy and life—makes the one who conquers a captain; the other—the conquered one, a servant, slave—what you will. It is so always, more or less. And in this marital duel there is no quarter; and, nine times out of every ten, it is the woman who holds the cards; she who wins. If she is clever, she knows this—knows the game is in her hands. But the dice she has to throw is her sex, and she has only been allowed one throw! And when she has thrown wastefully—Yes, it is here that disaster enters into marriage and makes tragedy of the game of life.

But there is another side—and a side that is of immense importance to women.

Undeniably the greatest function of any man in the life of the average woman is to be the father of her child. All other things he means to her are secondary to this. For this reason, after the birth of her first child, she frequently ceases, though she does not know it, to love her husband as a man, and for himself.

The feeling of a child against a woman's bosom is more to her than the kiss of a lover or the devotion of a husband. What is it that she feels? It is a liberating power; a sensation of unaccustomed unity—like a strong tide that carries her over everything, makes her unconscious of the worry of the days. It is life itself. It irradiates all the world about her, all that belongs to her—her very soul. She has become one with life—a creator, as a god.

That is why so often the man—the husband and the father, finds himself left outside this charmed circle of life.

And even when the marriage is childless (as happens most frequently in the marriages that come to the divorce courts), this same passionate, grasping maternity acts—indeed, acts sometimes with added fierceness and even more disastrously. She mothers her man, but she does not love him. She gives him the protection that she should have given to her children but she holds back the inspiration and the spur that he most needs from her.

The woman's life so often is filled with attending her children or her husband, whom she loves (I must press this home again), where she has no children, not as a mate, but as a child. She ceases to consider him as a man—to belong to him as completely as he belongs to her.

She holds back more and more of herself—the vital part that he wants, while, at the same time, she demands more and more from him. The man feels that he is losing, giving up his individuality with all that he cares for most, and, after a period of loneliness and unhappiness, broken, probably, with some bluster and conflict, he gives in and begins not to care.

The result in the end is almost certain. The lower types of husband from time to time, will break away and find compensation in wild love. Some will seek distraction in work, or will develop a temper and nerves. Other men of more refinement will suffer much more, till they too break away at last; they will turn from the reality of life to dreams, unless they too seek and find love and sympathy with some woman, who, without the binding security of marriage, is more careful to understand them and to love them for themselves.

Most wives have yet to learn the deeper responsibilities of love; and this not at all in regard to their duties to their husbands, which most often are too perfectly fulfilled, but in the more intimate and far more exacting task of giving them spiritual freedom as well as sympathy and understanding.

I believe that this failure on the part of so many wives, in holding back just what the man most craves and seeks for, is the real cause, to which all other causes are subsidiary, of that failure in the continuance of the husband's love, which brings so many marriages, which started in happiness, to the disaster of the divorce courts.

In my opinion, the greatest cause of error is in women's limited experience which makes their judgments hard. While another cause arises from the tendency, and already I have emphasised more than once (a tendency due to a deep inner cause of sex difference) to throw the whole blame for sexual sins upon men. Some women carry sex antagonism like a flag, which they flourish in every wind. These are, of course, a small minority, but the majority of women fail to take a wide, sane view both on this question of the unfaithfulness of husbands and that of the whole physical relationship of marriage.

And the remedy? Yes, that is the difficult matter. We cannot alter these inharmonies of love by any cut-and-dried reforms. The expression of sex is a question largely of understanding. Its regeneration must begin with a movement, in particular, on the part of women, towards a truer acknowledgment of their own natures and an acceptance of men's needs.

I dare to think of such a regeneration of Love, but it must come through education in consciousness and a fuller understanding of life. And by education must be understood all that influences the unconscious as well as the conscious self, so that our full life may be lived in harmony, and not with one half of ourself in enmity with the other half.

WHY WIVES ARE UNFAITHFUL

It may, and I expect will, be said that I am looking at this question of faithfulness in marriage from the man's side only. This is not because I do not see and sympathise with the woman's position. I am thinking really just as much of one partner as of the other. What I wish to do is to focus attention. For this reason, I am insisting upon the fact, of the wife's coldness as being most often the first cause which drives the husband from his affection and his duty. I do this because it is just the real cause that is almost always neglected, unrealised, in particular, by women themselves.

Women have been taught to believe, and do really feel, that by sexual unfaithfulness a husband does them the cruellest possible wrong that a man can do to a woman.

It is rare to find a woman who is not sexually jealous. To possess and to hold, even when she has ceased to desire the possession, is a quality that is exceedingly common in wives. And our iniquitous divorce laws, with their obsession with sexual offences, help to maintain this view of marriage.

But is the man ever wholly to blame? It is so easy to talk self-righteously of the unfaithfulness of men—of their polygamous nature and their attraction to wild love.

I never heard such nonsense. Men are the most faithful creatures alive. After all, almost in every case, the man has given away only what his wife has shown him she does not want for herself. As long as she desires him, indeed, often, *as long as she will put up with him*, her man will stick to her—yes, *stick with the closeness of the proverbial burr*.

Most English wives always are acquiescent, rather than passionate in the sexual embrace. Even when in love, they are shy and often unresponsive. Hiding what they feel, rarely showing their husbands that they want them with any real desire. Then, after a few years of marriage, his embraces are either evaded or repulsed, if not, they are *suffered as a duty*.

Everyone who does not blink facts, knows that the vast majority of marriages are unhappy owing to the coldness of the wife. Very often this starts from the beginning of marriage. The wife is disappointed: she finds the husband different from the lover of her dreams.

In the story of *Beauty and the Beast* we have material out of which part of the great sex difficulty can be explained. In the fairy story, the husband, who before marriage looks like a beast, after marriage, becomes a prince. In real life the story is inverted. There is a deluding force in the mere skin and limbs of those of the opposite sex at the time when maturity is reached which may give princely attributes to those who would be seen as beasts at other times. The prince seen as a beast after marriage is a tragedy into which the romantic, ignorant girl must beware of drifting. The man who most boldly plays up to the romantic part expected of him, reciprocating to the perhaps unconscious encouragement of the girl—is not the man who will be most agreeable to live with. I believe there is real danger in the sentimental view of love that is common to most girls. They do not know the poverty of feeling that loudly expressed sentiment may hide. The defect of many unfaithful lovers is not sensuality, but sentimentality. The lower types of lovers are strangely, almost incredibly sentimental.

It cannot, I think, be denied that sexual anaesthesia is present in many women and there would seem to be evidence that even where it is not present before experience of love, it arises *after marriage*. Any number of wives are unable to give themselves up to the sexual act in such a way as to derive from it real satisfaction and the gladness and health that it should give. This is a very grave matter. The evil would be less if these frigid women did not marry, but as a rule they do marry. It is a curious fact that women who sexually are cold, are sought as wives with greater frequency than are more passionate women, probably because their easily maintained reserve acts as a stimulus to the man's desire. Men are persistently blind in these matters. They want response to their own love in their wives, but most of them are very much afraid of any woman who possesses the strong passion to enable her to give such response.

In short, as we found in the previous essay on unfaithful husbands, woman gains her fulfilment from the man when he gives her his child. But when she turns from him, she leaves him unsatisfied. The drama and the novel are burdened with this problem, which, indeed, intrudes itself on every hand.

We have, by our wrong ideals, for long been inducing an entirely perverted view, which regards physical desire as something of which women should be ashamed, and the sex act as a thing in itself degrading and even disgusting—the nasty side of love and of marriage, something to be submitted to, indeed, in order to bear children or for the sake of the loved man whose passions must be allowed, but not a thing for health and desire—for the delight and perfection of the woman herself.

This false view, I affirm again, is the blight that has been, and still is, the destroyer of sexual happiness and health. And this fear and denial of love; this separation between the passion allowed to the man and not allowed to the woman, is the serious side of this problem of marriage. For the hideous disguises and constant lying, too often made necessary to both the partners, owing to the wife's entire failure to realise the physical necessities of love, makes domestic life an organised hypocrisy.

We fight and fight to be free. Yet ever the concealed antagonism lays fresh hold, upon both the husband and the wife. It crops up in many and curious ways, imposing its poison and destroying life—the deep, deep-hidden rage of unsatisfied love.

The need for love will not often allow itself to be inhibited without claiming payment. And if desire so frequently manifests itself in abnormal forms of the coarsest and commonest dissipation, this is almost always to be explained by some hindrance opposed to its normal expression. When women face facts and realise this truth, many things in the conduct of husbands will be clear that hitherto have been hidden from them.

There is, however, another aspect of this question which now must be considered. For to leave the matter here would be the greatest injustice. A further question must first be asked. Why is this coldness in women so prevalent? Why does the desire of even the loving wife so often cease towards her husband? It is a difficult question to answer. One reason has been given already. We have noted women's false attitude to love; an attitude which, in so many cases, makes her ashamed of expressing openly the passions she feels. Yet there is, I think another and much deeper part of the truth that is fairly clear. Love is a more difficult thing for women than it is for men. Each man is able to enforce his sexual desire upon his wife *at a time when she feels no desire, whereas she cannot gain her desire unless he gain his*. We may, perhaps, trace back to this cause, many of the feelings of disharmony and waning of desire which injures the woman's power to love.

I must follow this a little further. In marriage the husband, usually exercises his marital privileges *when he wishes*. He does not think sufficiently of, or understand sufficiently as he should, the wishes of his wife. For what *she says* must never be accepted as representing really what she wishes. It is very hard for any man to understand how almost impossible it is for a woman, if she is good, to be frank about sexual desire. Both our laws, and opinion and custom have strengthened the view—not usually openly acknowledged but usually felt—that the husband has the right to approach his wife when he desires. Her right is not equally considered, too often it is taken for granted that she has no desires or real sex-needs to be considered.

The result is inescapable. The man's passion finds relief while she remains unsatisfied. She is in just the same position as someone who is forced to eat a meal without appetite.

And inevitably this leaves her unresponsive, makes her irritable, capricious, and quite incomprehensible to her husband.

Of course, this disharmony, is not always conscious even to the woman herself, who usually fails quite to understand what is the matter or to connect her restless unhappiness with the stirrings of her unsatisfied love. The dyspeptic does not know that he wants food: he turns away from it. In the same way the woman turns away from love. She gives in to the inhibiting influences and accepts the abysmal misconception into which one sex has fallen in regard to the other.

This difference in the power for sexual sacrifice between the two sexes is, I have frequently thought, one of the gravest causes of misery in marriage. It will take very long to over come it. Only as we advance in refinement and knowledge of love can this antagonism in the sex act lessen, as the woman gains in frankness and the man comes to know how to arouse and keep aflame her desire.

For woman is passionate. There is no greater lie than the so often reiterated assumption that she *"is naturally and organically frigid."* 4 We must remember that this view of woman's coldness in love is of comparatively modern growth. Yet it is a lie that will take a real revolution in our moral ideas to uproot. It is, in large measure, at least, the result of our pretences—the horrible, grasping, destroying, back-wash of shams. It is the result of the way in which women have lived, with blinds drawn down on most of the unruly disturbance and elemental forces in love.

The wife whose love is turned away from her husband finds substitute satisfaction in her home and her children, if she has them, or, failing these, in dress and amusement and other outside interests; or in a lover, who gives her new hope of finding satisfaction in love. And the poor bewildered husband is quite unaware of the cause of this coldness. He cannot understand his wife's unfaithfulness. He does not know that his unthinking acceptance of her subordination to his desire, however gladly given, is what has, and indeed must, exhaust the passion in her.

For I do not deny, as already I have stated, that sexual coldness is exceedingly common on the part of the wife to-day. What I do deny is that this is a natural condition; rather is it a symptom of the mistakes of our civilisation that have cheated women and men alike of health and happiness in love.

I affirm again, that this idea of coldness in love being natural to women is entirely false. Complete absence of satisfaction in love cannot be borne, especially when living in the close intimacy of married life, by any woman, through a period of years, without producing serious results on the body and the mind. It is in the blighting effects of this pseudo-celibacy that we must seek the cause of the sterility of so many married women's lives.

Do I put this other side of the problem of marital-celibacy—the woman's side—in a strong light. Yes I do, but I put it faithfully as I have come to know it from the facts I see daily around me.

It is hard to say how often, and how many wives have put from them the temptation to seek happiness in love *at any price*; no less hard is it to compute to what extent the transformation of this suppressed sexual passion is expended in passion in other channels. We see it in a hundred cases to-day. In every instance where passion is called for woman tends by her nature to be carried further than man.

There is, of course, no exact measuring in these matters, but who among us can dare to say that the harm done by the deprivation of love is greater in the lives of men than of women? I doubt not it is the other way. We hear so much of the sex-needs of husbands that we have become a little wearied. We accept so much for them as being right and natural, but who shall calculate the number of equally right and natural impulses that women have resisted?—resisted until the very instinct to love tends in time to become dulled and blighted.

I am willing to grant, indeed, that few women experience that obsessing longing of the man to grasp the woman of his desire, nor do they, as a rule, I think suffer the same terrible physical depression that causes incapacity for control. I am not certain here: women are less open about these matters than men are, and one hesitates to judge other women by oneself. We are dealing with a question very difficult to solve. We may find some explanation in the fact that many passionate women have had to learn how the energy of the sexual impulse may be diverted into other activities. It is a lesson that possibly men will have to learn. Yet I do not know, the price women have had to pay has been heavy and the results gained very poor. And does not this denial of love entail a waste of life?—that is what really matters. It is very hard to know the truth.

Here, then, is the question I would put to men who are suffering to-day from the unfaithfulness of women. I would ask them. Have they taken sufficient trouble to understand, both on the physical and psychical side, the sexual nature of woman, which is much more complex than their own? The art of love is not understood by men. If they paid more attention to this subject marriage would be freed from the strongest and most frequently operating cause that brings it to disaster. But this will never be done until we have ruled out from our moral conscience the idea of "the body as the prison of the soul."

I have often asked myself if this misconception is not the real cause of all sex trouble?

SHOULD DOCTORS TELL?

Of the many differing opinions concerning the question whether doctors should reveal medical secrets, none that I know have been more interesting, in particular to women, than that of a local practitioner (whose name I have forgotten) who spoke at a Conference of doctors met to consider this question. In opposing with admirable frankness a resolution for the continuance of the practice of professional secrecy, he asked the straight question, whether "a bounder" should be allowed to live and his wife and child to die?

For here we touch at once the grave difficulty of the position. The discussion, as is evident, was concerned more particularly with the position in regard to venereal diseases.

The whole question has, indeed, been brought before public attention in connection with the recommendation of the Royal Commission on Venereal Diseases that a communication made by a medical practitioner with regard to these diseases and to guard the innocent from infection should be regarded as a privileged communication, and the law of libel be so modified as to give this safeguard.

Now, on the face of it, this would seem a simple matter. And the question I want to ask is, why the professional medical voice of this country has pronounced so emphatically against it? I know, of course, the reason that is given, that the divulging of a patient's secret, without his or her consent, and even if for a good reason, must weaken confidence—not only the patient's confidence in the particular doctor who "told," but the confidence of the public in the whole medical profession.

I do not think this reason bears any close investigation. Confidence is destroyed quite as surely, though probably not so quickly, by suppression of truth as by revealing it.

No, I believe we have to look deeper for the reason to explain this attitude of medical hiding.

These diseases are set apart from all other sicknesses of our bodies. For this reason, in considering them, moral considerations become confused with practical values. And I do not see quite how this is to be avoided. There is however, the gravest danger from such an attitude which rests upon hidden personal prejudices, and is not dependent on the facts of the case. Such an attitude leads inevitably to concealment of truth, which is specially disastrous here, because it is absolutely essential that these diseases, if they are to be cured, should be met in the open and grappled with methodically and thoroughly.

For greater clearness, I may state the matter thus: There are three attitudes that may be adopted towards sexual disease. First, that of the pure moralist, who says only "This is a sin to be punished." On the opposite side is the purely utilitarian, who says, "This is only a disease to be cured." But both attitudes may be alike wrong or, more correctly, the truth lies midway between the two. The disease, as a disease, needs to be cured. This is the first step with which nothing should interfere. But far different and much more complex is the treatment required to alter the actions that lead to the disease.

As a first step, public opinion ought to condemn too late marriage, instead of recommending it on economic grounds. The mania for making economics the deciding factor in conduct should surely cease: the falsity of this view has been exposed by many great writers, but much stronger is the condemnation that must be given here by all who can understand the evils that it has wrought in our sexual lives. Late marriages must be one of the causes contributing to men's use of prostitutes before marriage.

We have to find a way out, to silence our shrieks of blame, and to give up many of our old pretences. You can never get things right until you honestly face them.

Women are the worst sinners. And I say, without hesitation, that it is men's fear of women, especially the husband's fear of his wife, that is the greatest hindrance to openness in this connection. It is women's attitude which holds us back in progress towards health.

Let me give an illustration. I attended recently a meeting where a paper was read on the morals of men, in connection with the alarming increase of venereal diseases since the war. The reader of the paper, being a woman doctor as well as a feminist, took the wise view that the most urgent question was not the reform of the men, but staying the spread of the diseases. In the discussion that followed it was plainly evident that few of the audience—all women—agreed with her. These were women workers, who had read about, and to some limited extent, at any rate, thought and studied, these questions. Yet the general view was that men ought to be punished. One speaker, who stated that she was married, said that no true woman could or ought to forgive a husband who had become infected with a contagious disease.

Now, it is this view, here so crudely expressed, that has done so much harm in the past. It explains also the continuance of the medical secrecy that has acted so strongly against the stamping out of this scourge of civilisation. Such an attitude of blame and unforgiveness on the part of women has to be changed before the truth can be told safely.

Women are mainly responsible for the secrecy of these diseases. And what is the result? Because these infectious diseases are secret they are largely uncured.

It is, of course, easy to understand the attitude taken up by women. Blame of men is not easily avoided; yet is there not confusion in women's minds?

The sin that a husband commits against his wife, a man against the girl he is to marry—yes, and a son against the trust of his mother—is in being unfaithful. Having caught the disease is a misfortune. The effect must not be blamed by itself.

Let me illustrate this point of view by considering a different case. Your child gets scarlet fever by an act of direct disobedience—the sin of his age. He stays from school, without leave of absence, and goes to play at a house he has been forbidden to enter. Would you, because of his disobedience, refuse to pity and nurse him? Rather, would you not forget his sin and desire only to help and heal him?

Do you see what I mean now? It is not that I would condone immoral conduct in the husband or the lover that I plead for pity and understanding on the part of women who love them.

Few men are intentionally evil. They do not even always act foolishly in this question of infectious diseases because they are wantonly careless. Often they are fully alive to the danger that may result to their wives, or the girl they wish to make their wife, from their own infection.

I repeat, they are not necessarily bad men, and they love their wives and children; but they are cowards. All men are cowards when it comes to facing the blame and misunderstanding of the woman they love.

If they cannot rely on the woman's pity and help, few men will dare to tell the truth; nor will they be willing to let the doctor tell the facts for them. And if the truth cannot be told, it is very unlikely that the infection will not be spread to others. This may lead to the birth of diseased children, and who may say that in this case the crime is the man's alone?

Why can't we face the situation now, when we are trying to tidy up our social life? Concealments that may have been necessary in the old time of ignorance are surely impossible now.

Is the evil to remain hidden, uncorrected, from one generation to another? Hidden evil multiplies itself, and the sum is national deterioration.

The mistake has been the muddleheaded thinking that has obscured the plain and comparatively simple question of cure with the entirely opposed problem of moral appraisement and punishment: a confusion and losing of the way that has led us all inevitably into a forest-tangle of difficulty, of lies and silences, and unanswerable questions.

And this heritage of wrong thinking is still compassing our feet, binding them and throwing us down, as soon as we try to move a step onwards: and until that entanglement is broken through, by bringing the whole complicated position into the light of understanding and honest thinking, the evil will go on, unchecked by our futile tearings here and there at withered branches. The supporting stem of concealments and dishonesty will flourish, and the devastating evil will continue to spread.

THE MODERN WIFE AND THE OLD-FASHIONED HUSBAND

The old-fashioned husband is always older than his wife. If he is not old in years, he is old in character. His desires and instincts are aged. She is young because she is alive.

He wants to give her advice, but she will not listen. He desires to guide her, or he must think that he does so. He protects her. Thinks of her as young and precious and tender. He does not speak of certain things before her. He caresses her, he pays her bills, gives her presents, and treats her in the way, in which she has learnt not to treat her children.

For the old-fashioned husband is conservative and hopelessly romantic.

The fact is he ever seeks in his wife the image of his mother, the first woman whom he worshipped, and whose virtues remain as an unforgettable pattern, ever to be repeated. He sees her darning socks (horrible and useful occupation), making beds, dusting the china, arranging flowers, brushing her husband's overcoat and smoothing his hat, fussing needlessly over everything. These pictures are always interfering with the image of his wife—the new woman of to-day, with her restless and noisy movements, her slang and violence, her knowledge, capable management and clearness of vision-that-look-you-straight-in-the-eyes air that belongs now to wives.

Why have women altered so greatly? Why have women gone on and left their husbands behind?

It is common to refer everything back to the war. Certainly the war did this—it sent both women and men into difficult schools but the men's school was harder and quite different from that of the women.

If the war had a devastating effect, the peace has likewise had for women its revolutionary consequences. We all know what the war did. It took women out of their homes. The feminists rejoiced to see women in munition factories, on the platforms of trams, squeezed into government offices, hoeing and driving the plough. Then the peace threw them back; closed the open doors, cut off the day of financial prosperity, re-introduced them to their children, if they had any, and to their husbands.

And now what happened? What effect had this on the desires of women and men?

Why, the husbands yearned for the old order of home and wife and children. For the men had fought, they had experienced the uttermost bitterness of life. Their petrified imagination had had no new ideals. They wanted nothing changed. For them a terrible interlude was over, a nightmare passed, that must be forgotten. But the non-combatant women had not experienced war; they had only looked on. For many of them a glamour of patriotic achievement in various kinds of work, which they much preferred to the old domestic duties, added to the lure of high wages, had thrown a cloak of romance over the war-period. They had nothing to forget. The last thing they wanted was to go back, all their desire was set on going forward.

Here then, is the reason why to-day there are so many modern wives with old-fashioned husbands.

These war-trained women are very efficient; they impose their will on everyone; they are attractive and very honest, but sometimes rather aggressive with their assurance and massed information. They go to and fro from their homes, when they like and how they like. The husband knows almost nothing of his wife's friends. He supposes it is all right. But he understands that he cannot stop her, cannot control her interests. She makes his house her home, is his friend and dear companion, but she does not stay in his charge. Often he feels like a stranger, helpless, not knowing what to do.

Wives are now almost more independent than husbands used to be. "I want to do it, therefore, I must do it," is their acknowledged cry. They are on such good terms with life and with themselves that they cannot imagine another view—the old view of the woman sacrificing herself. There are quite a lot of things they won't do; they are very simple and straightforward about them.

Nowadays it is not fashionable for even young unmarried girls to remain in the guarded shelter of the home. Old-fashioned fathers and brothers, are sometimes alarmed at the freedom of friendship allowed—the light-hearted pairing off. Life is a game, a dance, like the figure in the lancers where you "visit" and waltz away, but then come back to do the same thing with another partner. Yet these girls are not without hearts; but they realise that they must know men before they can choose the one man to whom they may give themselves. They have almost nothing in common with the boneless emotional heroines of the past. They are very practical and know that love will not pay the baker's bills, and after realising all this, they have schooled themselves not to fall in love carelessly.

They look all life squarely in the face, understand their duties, what they will do and will not do, in a way that may be hard, but is admirably sane and admirably honest.

Here is an incident. An exceedingly modern girl was engaged by some ill-chance to an old-fashioned man. She came once to talk with him of her future and his. She was not fond of children and therefore, thought she ought not to have any. Gently he placed his hand over hers, "That will be as God wills, my darling." She sprang from him, "It won't, Ronald, that's not true, it will be as I arrange."

It used to be so different. The old-fashioned girl could never have spoken with such frankness. Wife or maid she was always younger than the man she loved. She studied him, listened to him, quoted him. She lived only in and through him. *At least that is what he thought.* He did not know that she did not really listen, was tired of his stories, not interested in his business or his friends. All her seeming submission and acceptance were used to hold him.

The opinions of the old-fashioned woman were quotations from authority; her motto was obedience, but her practice was sweet rebellion. Very rarely was she honest. Her eyes were so blinkered that she saw nothing that she did not wish to see.

No, I am not sorry for old-fashioned men. They remain so childishly blind. Let them grow up, or at least, conceal their paleolithic ideas.

The new types of modern women face the future with laughter and the present with quickly responsive feeling. They give still to the world the essential gift of the eternal feminine, though they are cutting away the worn-out unreasonable exaggerations of perverted femininity—the coldness of the vicious woman, the unkindness of the grabbing woman, the ignorance and submission of the old-fashioned good woman. They are able to see everything and to help in everything, without being deceitful, without being dulled.

THE TEMPORARY GENTLEMAN AND HIS YOUNG WIFE

Everyone is busily trying to explain why there are so many unhappy marriages at the present time, but few people seem to realise that one of the most prolific causes has been the comparatively recent tendency of women to marry out of their class. We all know that all social distinctions were in abeyance during the war, and even afterwards. Normal class separations, conventional standards, old careful habits of conduct have been largely broken through at a time of great uncertainty and many changes.

Some of us hoped that this new co-operation which seemed to be springing up between men and women of different social classes would lead to permanent changes. We forgot that excitement is the most potent intoxicant, and that after excitement there is usually a falling back into dullness and apathy. But certainly for a time there was quite a new loosening of the guiding-rein of reason, that has allowed the horses of impulse and instinct freer than ever before to pull the car of ourselves and our fates in this direction and in that, just as they chose.

The many misfit marriages bear witness to the excited condition of women.

And it ought not to be difficult to realise, with the least gift of imagination, the conflict and the unhappiness, almost necessarily resulting, from such unions, entered into during that period of topsy-turvy conditions, between the man who had "risen" and the more complicated type of modern girl—the girl of brains and nerves, passionate, intellectually emancipated and delighting in her new-gained freedom; yet, at the same time, fastidious, ruled by traditions and inherited habits, which crop up unexpectedly, with a conservatism that is neither acknowledged nor reckoned with.

The men who in commerce or in war had a meteoric success have, in many cases, fallen back; they are but clerks, shop-assistants, artisans. They themselves, and everything belonging to them seem different. While they were accepted as gentlemen, because of what they had done or the money they had made, they married "above them" as the phrase is. And now when the money is spent and what they did no longer remembered, they cannot find work that will enable them to maintain the outward show of being a gentleman. The intoxication of excitement is over, and their wives complain, not only of their position, but of them.

The temporary gentleman and his young wife, in many cases, are finding that it needs a lot of grit and a lot of duty to keep in love. For the rose-coloured glasses of courtship have been replaced by the blue goggles of matrimony. They are already unhappy, though they expected happiness. You see, their love has been tested by the love-destroying test of poverty. And these difficult days have cast their homes into disorder.

We have all felt the world's wave of trade depression: the world's difficulties have dealt a blow, causing a leak to spring in many a frail boat of domestic happiness, so that its inexperienced navigators no longer can exercise control over the journey.

Now it is customary to blame the wife. Always it is the woman's fault. She is, or ought to be, the home-maker. While no one seems to consider how much depends on the character, or conditions, of the home she is asked to make.

The boarding-school-educated and college girl has never been trained to perform or to endure the difficult, necessary duties of the poor man's home. In their girlhood's homes and luxurious schools, everything was done for them. That was in the old, almost-forgotten days of cheap domestic service.

In no other direction, perhaps, has there been so great and so far reaching changes as in the homes of the so-called upper classes. In a sense, to-day we have no homes, only places in which we sleep, and sometimes eat. For the domestic work of preparing the food and keeping the home as a place to live in and not to escape from has, in great measure, ended; duties which once it was every woman's pride to do well, have been allowed to slip, as far as possible, into the hands of hired experts. In the old days cooking and housekeeping, and even house-cleaning, were known to all women. Every wife was expected to enter into competition with other wives in the important matters of making bread and cakes, and in making jams and jellies and puddings.

But the home, with its old full activities, has passed out of the hands of the mistress. So to-day a girl often finds herself forced to learn the very elements of the routine day of the wage-earner's wife. And the duties that have to be learnt are many of them disagreeable as well as immensely tiring and monotonous to unaccustomed hands.

I do not, however, believe that the knife-and-fork aspect of these marriages is the fundamental aspect. It is love itself that is at fault. The strain and the jar of daily living under these difficult restless conditions have been too great, especially for the women.

The passing from one way of living, from one station of society to another, is always a hard and unpleasant process. We do not always know it or admit it, even if we *do know*, but the small, almost unnoticed differences in habits and manners are harder to tolerate than many a more fundamental cleavage.

I want to labour this point. The most frequent causes of trouble in those marriages where there is poverty and a restricted life, are born, I am certain, out of the daily fret of uncomfortable and cheap living together, out of small ugly minor habits of omissions, and stupidities.

Romantics may deny this, but what most wears and frays the love of wives are just trifles so small that very rarely is their adverse action directly noticed. But they give an escape for the concealed hostility, and set up an almost indecent and fearfully intolerant irritation. Dirty finger nails, the murdering of words, or making a noise when you eat soup, may be much harder to bear than real unkindness and anger. The failure to rise and give up a chair or to open a closed door may seem greater neglect to a wife than the absence of money to buy presents. The roughness of the "rough diamond" becomes unbearable. Things that once did not seem to matter, now matter tremendously.

Of course this is illogical, but then love is illogical.

And month by month as it passes makes the marriage more broken. The disappointment goes deeper though the irritation may, perhaps, be less frankly expressed. This is the time of the real danger. It is the wife's own love that is failing her, much more than anything her husband may do or not do.

The difficulty of finding suitable work, the differences in friends and in the accustomed spheres of life, could be overcome were it not for the *unconscious want of will to overcome them*. The man may feel that he would do better farming in Canada than here. It is a very certain indication that the woman has ceased to love him wholeheartedly if she objects to accompany him on the ground that all her friends are in England.

Love does not hesitate: it delights to give up and to sacrifice.

You will see what this means: It is rather the *hidden feelings that make conscious social difference*, that act and are far stronger than the difference itself.

The unacknowledged failure in Love, not anything that happens outwardly, is the real trouble that gnaws at the root of content in their marriages, and rots and breaks the bond.

Yet there is a bright side to these marriages even when they fail. The socially adventurous, the breakers of conventions, must expect trouble; but they may console themselves by reflecting that they are pioneers in opposing dead traditions. Only the tall trees sway in the breeze, the dwarf plants are ingloriously safe.

IS MARRIAGE TOO EASY?

On the subject of marriage I have written again and again, not alone in these essays, but in many of my other books. I would, however, wish to say now, and with all the power I have, that in England, marriage is made too easy. If some of the restrictions which are placed against the breaking of the marriage bond were transferred to the time when the bond is made it would be well.

We prevent too late. Always we run to shut the stable door after the horse is stolen.

Many amazing marriages are made, in particular, by the very young who to-day refuse, more fiercely than even before, any guidance from the old; reckless marriages, entered into by those who have known each other for a few days only before marrying for life.

An ever-increasing freedom and independence for the young has certainly had rather a startling moral result. It has been shewn that for all ordinary young men and women intimate association with each other in college, in business, in workshops, and factories, and in play, turns them with extreme readiness to love making. Now I am very far indeed from wishing to apportion blame, but I do hold that new conditions demand—not only changes in our thoughts and judgment, but revision of the laws formulated to restrict conduct.

A minister of religion stated publicly, not very long ago, "I have had to marry many couples who admitted to me they knew little about each other. I could do nothing. I was not allowed to refuse marriage."

The many marriages made in haste and under the pressure of sudden emotional urgencies, are a sign of the nervous condition of the times. The customary criticisms of reason are not heard, or not until the emotional storm has subsided. This is, of course, a condition not infrequent in love, but in these rushing and exciting days of dancing-partners and jazz courtships, it is greatly exaggerated, such marriages may not unfortunately bear the scrutiny of minds restored to reason. Living together is found to be a different and far harder thing than dancing together. And this has led to the unprecedented demand for divorce which should cause no surprise or lamentation, but should urge us forward to face the situation, like spurs in the flesh of a tired horse. For the disgrace is, not that these marriages should end, but that they should ever have begun.

We English are too afraid of preventative interference: we wait until something is very wrong indeed and then we punish.

It would be salutary for us to consider the more careful regulations of other lands. In France, for instance, and in Belgium no encouragement is given for hurried marriages such as we permit. Official enquiries and the consent of parents and guardians are considered necessary. From the start the greatest care is exercised. *Fiançailles* (engagements) are regarded as serious family events, more binding and more sacred than anything to which we are accustomed. Both the engagement and the marriage are affairs of the utmost importance to the two families concerned as well as to the young people themselves. There are discussions and careful arrangements, and months of testing of suitability for life-partnership, during which the future husband and wife get to know one another before being tied by marriage. Perhaps, this is why the crime of bigamy is very rare in France, and there is no such thing known as cases for breach of promise of marriage.

I know, of course, the many and great evils that are attendant on the French system, but to me it seems that these could easily be avoided as they arise entirely out of property considerations and the wife's dowry—considerations which so inevitably act disastrously on moral conduct.

It would, I am certain, lessen the chance of endless unhappiness in marriage and prevent many divorces if some more fixed inquiries, with—in the case of any one (shall I say, under twenty-five?) the consent of one parent of either party, if living, if not, that of a guardian, were obligatory before the marriage could be entered into. Or if the young will not accept this parental authority, marriage could be made conditional, except under very special reasons, on the betrothal months having lasted for a fixed and sufficiently long period: at least inquiry should be made as to the amount of knowledge the partners have gained of each other. I would recommend these reforms to all who are concerned for the future of marriage.

Nor need the change be difficult or would it entail any great alterations in the machinery of the law. We appoint a King's Proctor to inquire into domestic details to prevent unsuitable marriages being broken, why not change his duties to prevent unsuitable marriages being made?

I would urge also that Commandments of Marriage are formulated to be read to every couple at their betrothal and again before the wedding ceremony takes place, as is done to some limited extent in France and Belgium and in one or two other countries. This is another duty which might be undertaken by the department of the King's Proctor.

Here, then, is a practical way in which we might wisely copy other civilisations whose customs are more carefully planned to safeguard marriage and help the young in right living.

I must press home this question of the dangers of too easy marriage, though I risk wearying my readers by repetition. The facilities we give the young for marrying in haste, is, I affirm again, the cause mainly responsible in the greater number of marriages that come to the disaster of the Divorce Courts. This I have proved already. It is responsible also for many cases of bigamy, a crime which has increased alarmingly in the last years. Our law of breaches of marriage promises, with its frequent misuse and extortion of hushmoney, is another cause dependent on our stupid neglect to regulate marriage. It leads to many unsuitable marriages being made, which very often have their fatal sequel of separation or divorce.

Nor does the disaster end here. Our present careless laws are certainly acting to bring marriage itself to discredit. We hurry young people within its bonds, freeing them from all obligations to their families or to society in this matter of choosing their life's partner, and then later, if disaster overtakes them, with callous irony we say, "you have made your bed, you must lie on it."

If we desire really to preserve marriage, let us treat marriage with seriousness. As I have said in another of these essays—Marriage is not considered a vocation: it has become a game. I would urge practical and prompt action. We are, I think, bound to realise that if we are to succeed in freeing our society from the evils which all of us are deploring, our attention must shift from attempts to *punish after wrong has been done,* to removing the causes that *lead certainly to wrong being done.*

In other words we have to formulate more practical and helpful laws. Even more important is to change public thought, cleansing men and women from their desire to punish and replacing instead the desire to help and to understand. Nothing else, in my opinion, can avert even greater disasters of license in the future than those we are facing.

PASSIONATE FRIENDSHIPS

I had wished to write these essays without too frequent mention of the war. I find, however, that such avoidance is almost impossible. For the war has, in the most effective way, made prominent all the problems of sexual conduct with which I am dealing, has done this so effectively that some way out must be found. New and even startling changes have come and are coming, and have to be faced. Certainly our judgments can never be the same. Many who never before thought about these things have been made to think. All of us have seen more plainly the ineffectiveness of much that always before we had accepted. No longer can we cover our eyes with the comfortable mid-Victorian bandages. There has ended for every one of us our blind-man's-buff game with life.

We are caught: and it is well. The unwritten commandment of sexual conduct, that anything may be done as long as the doing of it may be hidden, can never, I think, again be accepted, unless, indeed, by the very good, whose entire lack of humour makes them able to accept anything.

Whether we like it or not most of us have got now to muck-rake into the dark bye-paths of conduct.

Now, it is easy to say that this urgent concern with sexual questions arises from decadence. I do not believe it. To me it has always seemed that this growing demand for inquiry affords the surest hope for the future. Much is being thrown on to the scrap-heap of life. This is done only when there is need for it. We, who have come to see and in some measure to understand, have got to be concerned with sex and its problems, until some of its wrongs are righted.

Here I must digress to make a necessary explanation. The special problem of sexual conduct which now I wish to consider—the very difficult problem of passionate friendships between men and women who, for one reason or another, are unable or do not wish to marry, is a question to which my interest has for very long been directed. I was first asked to write about it in 1913 (how remote that time now seems) in answer to two articles that had appeared in the *English Review*, in July and August of that year, *Women and Morals* and *Men and Morals*, supposed to have been written, the one by "A Mother," and the other by "A Father;" but which, as later transpired, were thought out and transcribed in the office, by the Editor and sub-Editor of that then courageous journal.

But to whatever journalistic trickery they owed their origin, the interest of those articles remained unchanged. I need not wait to describe them; their importance rested in the courage and truth with which they faced the difficult problem, at that time almost always hidden or sentimentalised over, of the sex-needs of men and women apart from marriage.

I was asked to answer—I had, as it were, to sum up, sift out, weigh and judge, what was said in both articles. I did not then know anything of their bastard authorship, and I accepted. My answer appeared in the September number of the Review. At the time it gained some attention. In America the three articles were republished together. The little book, called "Women and Morals" had an exceedingly attractive cover and an excellent preface: I believe it sold widely. More amusing and also, I think, more witness to the power of my work, was a very different kind of notoriety which, in one quarter at least, it achieved in this country. It aroused anger. The number of the *English Review* in which it appeared was, I believe, burnt publicly in an Advanced Club for women by order of the ladies who then formed the committee. For their intense virtue considered my views too horrible to remain uncleansed by fire. (Excuse my laughing, but the fact is I always do laugh when I picture this incident—those splendidly blinkered women holding solemnly in extended fire-tongs that burning review!)

My work was immoral!

Immoral! What is it that people mean? I do not know. I am for morality and always shall be. That is, indeed, why I offend. I am always wanting to turn out dirty places and to spring-clean life. And I have to show things as I find them, not as I would like them to be. It is so easy if you drug your soul and place blinkers over your intelligence. But you cannot be moral if you are over-occupied with being nice.

It is the young, not the old, who are thinking and writing to-day. Let me give you an example that exactly fits this question we are considering.

By a somewhat suggestive coincidence there appeared an article on "Youth and Marriage" in the *English Review* for May, 1923—the last number issued under the editorship of Mr. Austin Harrison—which very strikingly repeats, but more openly and with cruder emphasis, almost everything that was said in the three articles published in 1913. It treats the same difficult and still unsettled question of sexual relationships outside of marriage. The article gives the answer of youth to the old, who are criticising and condemning the friendships and new freedom of sex intimacy between young women and young men: they are told frankly that they fail to realise the changed conditions of present-day life. The name of the writer of this interesting article, Vera M. Garrell, is unknown to me, but I take this opportunity of thanking her. Her article has given me the greatest pleasure. All the facts are considered in a refreshingly candid, if not always entirely adequate way. (1) The increased enormous disparity between the numbers of the sexes, which the writer comments upon as "an outstanding tragedy of the war;" leading as it must do, to "an unhealthy competition to attract men," under the urge of which girls are drawn "to use coarser measures and act on bolder lines," if they are to escape "the dark dread that haunts the average girl of being 'left on the shelf.'" (2) The economic factors, which cause marriage to become increasingly difficult, and thus act in lowering the marriage ideal by making a permanent union so remote that it comes to be regarded as "practically impossible." "The young people of to-day are very much realists. They intensely dislike poverty." A great deal is said about this "economic blockade against marriage," and the writer maintains that "much of the laxity in sexual morals is the direct outcome of this position." (3) Yet, even deeper in their action are the inner reasons. War has left the youth of to-day "with a kind of sexual neurosis." For years it kept life "entirely physical;" "morality was at a discount," the inescapable result has been that "youth has been lured into sexual compromise." The old code of morality has failed: it does not meet the new demands.

I have been impressed and sharply hurt at the bitterness and fatalism underneath what is written. Let me quote one or two sentences. "The charge against youth is correct. He is in revolt against conventional morality. *Young men and young women are sex conscious, not on the old lines of retiring from intimacy, but rather in the opposite direction of intimacy.*" And again, "Every sex companionship is born of *mutual recognition of social grievances*. Where it is possible for men and women to come together and form friendships they do so, *without any regard for the commital convention that marriage must be the object*." (The italics in the passages are mine.)

It is insisted upon that every normal person has a right to self-expression in the sex-function, while further frank acknowledgement is made that when sex-friendship "*is unregulated it ends in vice*." "*We shall not marry so why not enjoy ourselves*," is the prevailing philosophy of those who have ceased to regard the sexual act as immoral. (Again the italics are mine).

Now, all this has set me thinking that it is worth while to restate certain propositions in connection with these friendships of passion, which I made first in the article I wrote in 1913. I do this for two reasons. First I would like to assure the young, who to-day are more than ever impatient of, and condemnatory of, the old, that the old are not always ignorant and that some of them, too, have tried honestly to face this difficult problem of sexual conduct. The second reason is deeper. A sickness of soul cries out from so much that the young say to-day. I want to end this. And the only way in which I know to do this in connection with these unregulated friendships is to *have them regulated*.

It is ridiculous to say as so many of the young do to-day that sexual relationships between two people affect no one but themselves, unless a child is born. It is not true. The partners in even the strongest and purest union have no right to say to society, "This is our business and none of yours." The consequences may be so grave and wide-reaching for society that the sex-deed can never be confined to the pair concerned.

And I would go further even than this. For the sexual partnership that is kept secret, almost of necessity, will work anti-socially. Just in the same way as in any other secret partnership, opportunity will be given to those who desire to escape from the responsibilities of the partnership. This inevitably leads to the commital of sin, by those who are weak and unfixed in character. While other men and women of higher conscience, who wish to, and would act honourably, often find the way so difficult that they fail in their endeavours—lose themselves in the dark and tangled ways of concealment. Many unions that now are shameful, would not have been shameful, if the partners had not been drawn into deceitful concealments, that cannot fail to act in a way disastrous to love.

This problem of Passionate Friendships, like all problems of sexual conduct, demands something more than emotional treatment; it requires the most careful consideration of many different sets of facts, that often rise up in what seem to be direct opposition.

I must follow this a little further. The sex-needs are almost always dealt with as though they stood apart and lay out of line with any other need or faculty of our bodies. This is, in part, due to secrecy which has kept sex as something mysterious. We have most of us been trained from our childhood into indecent secretiveness. There is as well deeper trouble, and it will be a long time before we can change it. Sex is so powerful in most of us, and occupies really so large a part of our attention, that we are afraid of ourselves, and this re-acts in fear of any open acknowledgement of our sex-needs.

It is necessary before we can even begin to judge this question of passionate friendships, to face very frankly this tremendous force of the sex-impulses, for the most part veiled in discussion. Next to hunger this is the most imperative of our needs, and, indeed, to-day sex enters more into conscious thought than hunger. For the hunger needs of most of us are satisfied, while the sex-needs are thwarted and restrained in all kinds of ways, and thus insist themselves the more insistently in our thoughts. Here is some slight explanation why so many of our judgments about sex are so arbitrary and so unforgiving. In penalising the sexual misconduct of others we are really passing judgment, though we do not know it, on our ourselves in blaming them we gain a curious kind of vicarious salvation, which brings the peace of self-forgiveness. In devising punishments for others, we are fixing a compensatory sacrifice for our deeply buried wishes, which never having found relief, either in direct expression or by sublimation, remain to torment us with ceaseless conflicts in our unconscious life.

I must not follow this further. Anyone with knowledge of the new psychology will understand what I mean.

Now, what I want to emphasise is that, to some limited extent at any rate, this system of self-concealments and lies is being broken, or if that view is too hopeful, at least the point of view has shifted. Indeed it is the acceptance of the imperative force of sex hunger, and the frank recognition of the present position—a fearless acknowledgment of the natural right of every adult woman as well as man to sex experience, that renders so noteworthy the change in outlook between this generation and the last. The youth of to-day have been fearless enough to cry aloud desires that the men and women of my generation, either denied or whispered about. Within its limits (and I am bound to say that, in my opinion, these limits are badly fixed and very narrow), this is the most truthful generation that yet has existed. I am glad to have lived to know it.

It is true that the many difficult problems of sexual conduct, of which we hear so much and so continuously, in almost every case are approached from one side only—the personal-pleasure side. That is why there is so much waste and foolishness. It explains too, why there is no consistent and united movement; no attempt at trying to find for everyone some possible decent way out—an escape from the terrible conditions which we are all agreed exist under the difficulties and strain of our under-controlled and over-civilised life.

A new conception of morality is, indeed, called for, but we have to be clearer as to what it is to be and where it is taking us. You will see at once what I mean. Until new safeguards are established, the old restriction cannot safely be loosened. It is too dangerous. The brief passionate partnership must entail disaster, in particular for the woman. She must still pay the heavier price of love. For what do these partnerships really mean? There can be no glossing with talk about freedom here. It is the old solution, the giving by the woman *without security*, what is given by the woman who is married under security and permanence.

I do not believe this can be accepted as an established and permitted thing as soon as we come to consider the lasting results.

It is an essential part of sexual morality, as I conceive it, that in any relation between the two sexes—I care not whether the association be legal or illegal, recognised or unrecognised—the position of the woman, *as the potential mother* must be made secure. This is a social, not a private matter. As such it has always been accepted by a wise State: it is the disgrace of our lax civilisation that too often to-day it is forgotten or ignored.

We come then to this—How can provision be made for honourable partnerships with *security for the woman* outside of marriage? For I am altogether persuaded that this provision must be made in order to harmonise our sexual life, and meet the desires of a large and increasing number of young people, whose exceptional needs our existing institutions and customs ignore or crush.

We must all of us know from our experience of life that many women as well as men are by their temperaments unsuited for monagonious marriage—the living permanently with one partner for life. Often, I would even say as a rule, these individuals are strongly sexual. They will not, because with the character they have, they cannot, live for any long period celibate. They will marry to gain permanent sexual relief or, if they are men, they will buy temporary relief from prostitutes, unless they are able to seek satisfaction in an irregular union.

Now, I affirm it as my conviction that the first and second of these courses are likely to lead to greater misery and sin than the third course; and of the three, the first, in my opinion, is the worst. I have, no doubt at all on this matter. No one, who is not blind to the facts of life, can close their eyes to the evil and suffering that certainly follows, when permanent marriage is entered into by those people who are unfitted *and do not desire* to fulfil the obligations and duties of living faithfully with one partner. And I would ask all those who stand in fear of change or reform, and cannot contemplate any open toleration of wider opportunities for sexual friendships to consider this fact: the discredit which has fallen upon marriage arises largely from the demoralising lives lived under its cover by those unsuited for enduring mating.

It is commonly taken for granted that love and passion in men is quite different from love and passion in women. I am sure this is not true. It is very necessary to break down the idea that for the impulses of sex, with their immense complications and differences, there is one general rule. Nor is it possible, I am sure, to make any for arbitrary judgments. To me the man or woman who is able to live in faithful love with one partner is not necessarily better than the man or woman who is not so able. I may prefer the one type, and dislike the other, but that again is a matter of personal judgment. We cannot safely class those who differ from ourselves as wrong, and set them down as fit only for suppression and education. We have to put aside the old shrieks of blame that are possible only to the ignorant.

It is all very well to preach the ideal of complete sexual abstinence until marriage, but there are the clear, hard conditions of contemporary circumstances for all but the really rich, who can marry when they want to do so without other considerations, and the very poor who marry young because they have nothing at all to consider. We have to face the presence among us to-day of an amount of suffering through enforced celibacy, which is acting in many directions in degrading our sexual lives. Any number of these sufferers, both the unmarried and the married who are ill-mated, are everywhere amongst us. I need not wait to prove this: the facts face us all, unless, indeed, we are too wilfully blind and too prejudiced to see what is happening.

I would propose as a first step towards honesty and health, that we ought to claim an open declaration of the existence of any form of sexual relationship between a woman and a man. We shall, I believe, have to do it, if not now, then later, because we are finding out the evils that must ensue, both to the individuals concerned and to the society of which they are members, by forcing men and women into the dark, immoral way of concealments.

I believe if there were some open recognition of these partnerships outside of marriage, not necessarily permanent, with proper provision for the woman and her children, should there be any, a provision not dependent on the generosity of the man and made after the love which sanctioned the union had waned, but decided upon by the man and woman in the form of a contract before the relationships were entered upon, there would be many women ready to undertake such unions gladly; there would even be some women as well as men, who, I believe, would prefer them to permanent marriage, which binds them to one partner for life and as a rule entails mutual living together and the giving up by the woman of her work or profession. In this way many marriages would be prevented which inevitably come to disaster. It is also possible that such friendship-contracts might, under present disastrous conditions, be made by those who are unsuitably mated and yet are unable or do not wish to entirely sever the bond between them, with some other partner they could love. Such contracts would open up possibilities of honourable partnership to many who must suffer from enforced sexual abstinence or be driven into hateful concealed intimacies.

I do not think we need fear to do this. My own faith in monogamous marriage, the living together of one man and one woman for the life of both, as the most practical, the best, and the happiest form of union for the great majority of people, is so strongly rooted that I do not wish, because I hold it unnecessary, to force anyone either to enter or stay within its bonds. I want them to do this because they themselves want to be bound. We get further and further away from real monogamy by allowing no other form of honourable partnerships.

Under present conditions and the prejudice of social opinion, the penalties that have to be paid in particular by women, for any sexual relationship outside of marriage are too heavy. This is manifest as I have, to some extent, pointed out already. Indeed when we consider the difficulties faced in these unions, that so many do take the risks is another proof, if one were needed of the elemental strength of the sex-impulse. But mark this: it is only those whose social conscience is for some reason unawakened who can enter into these irregular relationships except under special and very exceptional circumstances, until some steps have been taken to regulate them. They may be willing to take the risk for themselves, but they know, or perhaps I had better say *ought to know,* that the payment may fall also on the child of their love. You may say—there need be no children. This is true. It makes the conditions of such love much easier. It is not, however, a solution and can never, I think, be accepted as such by women. The woman who loves a man wants to be the mother of a child by him. I shall be told that there are women of whom this is not true. I know this. But that does not make it less true that the great majority of women can find the completion of their love only in the child.

It would, of course, be easy to raise any number of objections against these contract-partnerships, some of which might well prove true. It may be said, for instance, that the economic difficulties that now prevent marriage would not be lessened, but increased, by these extra-conjugal relationships. This is a question on which so much ought to be said that I feel compelled to say almost nothing, as I cannot now treat it adequately. I can only say that I have in my mind some scheme of insurance, which might easily be contributed to by both partners of the contract, but which would go to the woman for her own provision, and that of any children of the union in case of separation. If this once became established as a custom (a kind of marriage settlement, but without the marriage) necessary between all entering into such partnerships, the practice would gain the support of public opinion. It is done frequently now, but secretly. What I want is that it should be done openly, as a right and not a favour. It would then be possible to take another step in the form of State endowment for parenthood; this might be an extension of endowment for legal motherhood and mother's pensions, and by doing this would follow another and, perhaps, even greater gain. The recognition of these contract-partnerships would prevent the ostracism which even to-day falls on the discarded mistress. There are many women who dread this much more than poverty. The whole question of any sexual relationships outside of marriage in the past has been left in the gutter, so to speak. Everything has been blotted in darkness and made disgraceful by concealment. This would be changed.

May not something be done now, when in so many directions we are being forced to consider these questions, to establish sanction to meet new needs? Partnerships other than marriage have had a place as a recognised and guarded institution in many older and more primitive societies, and it may be that the conditions brought upon us may act in forcing upon us a similar acceptance.

We have got to recognise that our form of monogamous marriage cannot meet the sex-needs of all people. To assert that it can do this is to close our eyes to the known facts. Something has got to be done. The extending of the opportunities of honourable love must be faced before we can hope for more moral conditions of life. It is the results that have almost always followed these irregular unions that have branded them as anti-social acts. But the desertion of women with the inevitable resulting evils, which has arisen so frequently from the conditions of secrecy under which they now exist, would be put an end to. One reason why extra-conjugal relationships are discredited is because it is often almost impossible to avoid disaster. Make these partnerships honourable and there will be much greater chances of honourable conduct. I spoke just now of the sacrifice of women. But in love there is no such thing as sacrifice for a woman; there is the joy of giving. The sacrifice arises out of the conditions of concealment and blame under which the duties and joys of love so often have had to be fulfilled.

I do not see how we can forbid or treat with contempt any partnership that is openly entered into and in which the duties undertaken are faithfully fulfilled. It is our attitude of blame that has, in the past, so often made this honourable fulfilment of obligations impossible.

I have sought to put these matters as plainly as may be in the conviction that nothing can be gained by concealment. Anyone who writes on the subject of sexual conduct is very open to misconceptions. It is not realised that the effort of the reformer is not to lessen at all the bonds in any sexual partnership, rather the desire is to strengthen them. But the forms of the partnership will have to be more varied; unless, indeed, we prefer to accept unregulated and secret vice. We shall, I do most sincerely believe, have more morality in too much wideness than in too little.

I can anticipate a further objection that will certainly be raised. Why, I shall be asked, if sexual relationships are to be acknowledged and protected outside of marriage, preserve marriage at all? I have answered this question already. *Monogamous marriage will be maintained because the great majority of women and men want it to be maintained.* I affirm again my own belief in the monogamic union: the ideal marriage is that of the man and woman who have dedicated themselves to each other for the life of both, faithfully together to fulfil the duties of family life. This is the true monogony: this is the marriage which I regard as sanctified. But, I, regarding it as a holy state, would preserve it for those suited for the binding duties of the individual home so intimately connected with it.

The contract-partnerships I have suggested will do nothing to change the sanctity of any true marriages. There will always remain a penalty to those who seek variety in love, in that unrest which is the other side of variety. And the answer I would give to those who fear an increase of immorality from any provision for sexual partnerships outside of permanent marriage is, that no deliberate change in our sexual conduct can conceivably make moral conditions worse than they are at present. As a matter of fact every form of irregular union exists to-day, but shamefully and hidden. The only logical moral objection that I can think of being advanced against an honourable recognition of these partnerships is that, by doing away with all necessity for concealments their number is likely to be larger than if the old penalties are maintained. This is undoubtedly true: it is also true that it is the only possible way in which they can cease to be shamefull. Prohibitions and laws, however stringent, can do nothing. The past has proved their failure; they will fail still worse in the future.

Nor is the change really so great or so startling as at first it may appear to be. Our marriage in its present form is primarily an arrangement for the protection of the woman and the family. What I want is that some measure, at least, of the protection now given to the legal wife, shall be afforded to all women who fulfil the same duties. I am not seeking to make immorality easier; as I have before insisted, that is very far from my purpose. These changes for which I am pleading will make immorality much harder, for it will not be so easy as now it is to escape from the responsibilities of love.

No one can suppose, of course, that this change can be other than gradual. There will be no stage at which a large section of society will give up the accepted custom and stand perplexed as to how they shall readjust their sexual conduct. Any movement towards openness and honesty must be gradual. The process of change will be in the future, what has always happened in the past, the slow abandonment of worn-out conventions, and a trial of new paths, first by the few, to be followed by an ever-increasing number. When the need for a change arises then does a change come.

I assert again there need be no fear.

It is one of the deepest and healthiest instincts of men and women that they have always fought for liberty to love, and have rebelled whenever the restrictions and conditions of society have borne too hardly upon them. There is first a period of dull acquiescence, followed certainly by a reaction towards pleasure and sin—the grabbing to take what has been withheld by any means and in any form; but afterwards comes rebellion—

the true movement towards purity; the deep desire of a return to health, necessitating always the breaking through from all hindering barriers, so that the intolerable burden of sin may be cast; a glad imperative effort to gain liberty, to live rightly and joyously.

It is the young who to-day have a new consciousness of the right of freedom. They will never again accept the ancient restrictions. And it is well. We, who are older, whose steps are faltering and whose eyes grow dim with waiting for the vision we have seen, look to them to gain liberty, to re-establish the sanctity of love, which we have tried to do and failed.

But the young must shake off every symptom of the prevalent and contagious anaemia of fatalism that limits everything to the personal issues, before they can formulate and carry through any really constructive work of reform. They must learn to distinguish more clearly between cause and effect, the means and the end. At present they place the horse after the cart and mistake the power for the product. We are all apt to suppose conduct and feelings are the outcome of conditions and laws. They are not: they are the origin of them. When we have all got the desire for right and honourable conduct and honest conduct and honest feelings both about marriage and every form of sexual partnership, we shall get living and helpful laws.

What is the use of tinkering with what is moribund? A great teacher has said, "Let the dead bury their dead; come and preach the good and the new thing."

CONCLUSION

REGENERATION

I have dared to think of a regeneration of our sexual lives through education and a fuller understanding of the meaning of love. But by education must be understood all that influences the desires and imagination, so that in every direction we shall be turned to seek health and clean living.

Our supine acceptance of so many things that are wrong ought to arouse us to shame. What are we going to do?

Are we content to go on in the muddles that so long we have accepted without much consideration? Are we satisfied to allow all the evil to continue because we are too lazy and too dishonest to face them in truth and demand a clearance? We are all responsible; you, my readers, and I. If we demand saner and more practical conditions we shall get them.

But do we care—I mean care sufficiently to seek and to find the way of escape? Ah, that is the question!

Fear has been the hot-bed wherein have been forced rank plants of shame, dishonesty and trickery, of uncleanness, of concealments, of persecution and punishments—plants of persistent but unhealthy growth, that insistently and riotously spring up to hinder the workers, who strive ever to clear the soil of the fair Garden of Love, from the rank and choking growths.

What wonder, indeed, that we have lost our way so that still we are wandering in the jungle, unable to steer a straight course through the rough and tortuous paths left to us as a legacy from the past. It is this confusion that is hindering us to-day. And our real task is to cut through the jungle, and force clear paths, so that again we may have good roads in an open country on which we may walk gladly and fearlessly.

Yet, it were unwise to be too hopeful. We cannot be architects of life. Each generation will make new mistakes, even do they escape the follies that are old. We can see a very short way along the path of life, and often we are confused. The wisest amongst us are only bricklayers, and the best can but lay two or three bricks in a lifetime. Our work is to do that if we can. We can guess very feebly at the whole design. Many mistakes must be made by us, as they have been by those before us, and often it may be the duty of a new generation to pull down the work that in sorrow we have toiled to build up.

FOOTNOTES

1 The English Edition was translated from the French Edition.

2 See a most instructive pamphlet, "The Conflicts of the Child," by Edith and Dr. Eder, reprinted from "Child Study," 1917.

3 See the pamphlet to which already reference has been made.

4 This frequently quoted statement was made by Lombroso and not by Krafft-Ebing as almost everyone seems to think. It is significant that the women on the study of whose sexuality this judgment was founded were of the prostitute class. See *La Donna Delinquente*, etc., p.p. 54–56.

INDEX